COMMON COMMANDS FOR SENDING MAIL

INVOKING MAIL	
mail *user*	Start a message to the specified user
mail *user1 user2*	Start a message to the users specified
mail *user* < *file*	Mail the file *file* to *user*
mail *site!user*	Start a message to *user* at *site*

COMMANDS THAT AFFECT THE HEADER	
~t *user2*	Add *user2* to the recipient list
~c *user2*	Send a copy to *user2*
~b *user2*	Send a blind copy to *user2*
~s *subject*	Make *subject* the message subject
~h	Edit the message header

EDITING COMMANDS	
~v	Invoke the vi editor on the message
~e	Invoke the ed editor on the message
~p	Display the message so far

READING AND SAVING FILES	
~r *file*	Read the file *file* into the message
~d	Read the file dead.letter into the message
~w *file*	Write the message into the file *file*
Ctrl-D	Send the current message

LEAVING MAIL	
~q	Abort the current message
~!*command*	Escape to the shell and execute the specified *command*

Computer users are not all alike.
Neither are SYBEX books.

We know our customers have a variety of needs. They've told us so. And because we've listened, we've developed several distinct types of books to meet the needs of each of our customers. What are you looking for in computer help?

If you're looking for the basics, try the **ABC's** series. You'll find short, unintimidating tutorials and helpful illustrations. For a more visual approach, select **Teach Yourself**, featuring screen-by-screen illustrations of how to use your latest software purchase.

Mastering and **Understanding** titles offer you a step-by-step introduction, plus an in-depth examination of intermediate-level features, to use as you progress.

Our **Up & Running** series is designed for computer-literate consumers who want a no-nonsense overview of new programs. Just 20 basic lessons, and you're on your way.

We also publish two types of reference books. Our **Instant References** provide quick access to each of a program's commands and functions. SYBEX **Encyclopedias** provide a *comprehensive reference* and explanation of all of the commands, features and functions of the subject software.

Sometimes a subject requires a special treatment that our standard series doesn't provide. So you'll find we have titles like **Advanced Techniques, Handbooks, Tips & Tricks**, and others that are specifically tailored to satisfy a unique need.

We carefully select our authors for their in-depth understanding of the software they're writing about, as well as their ability to write clearly and communicate effectively. Each manuscript is thoroughly reviewed by our technical staff to ensure its complete accuracy. Our production department makes sure it's easy to use. All of this adds up to the highest quality books available, consistently appearing on best seller charts worldwide.

You'll find SYBEX publishes a variety of books on every popular software package. Looking for computer help? Help Yourself to SYBEX.

For a complete catalog of our publications:

SYBEX Inc.
2021 Challenger Drive, Alameda, CA 94501
Tel: (415) 523-8233/(800) 227-2346 Telex: 336311
SYBEX Fax: (415) 523-2373

Mastering UNIX
Serial Communications

Mastering UNIX

Serial Communications

PETER W. GOFTON

SYBEX ®

San Francisco ▲ Paris ▲ Düsseldorf ▲ Soest

Acquisitions Editor: Dianne King
Managing Editor: Barbara Gordon
Editor: Doug Robert
Technical Editor: Chris Durham
Word Processors: Lisa Mitchell, Ann Dunn, Deborah Maizels
Book Designer: Eleanor Ramos
Chapter Art: Lisa Jaffe
Technical Art: Delia Brown
Desktop Publishing Production: Len Gilbert
Proofreaders: Vanessa Miller, Patsy Owens
Indexer: Nancy Guenther
Cover Designer: Ingalls + Associates
Cover Photographer: Mark Johann

SYBEX is a registered trademark of SYBEX, Inc.

TRADEMARKS: SYBEX has attempted throughout this book to distinguish proprietary trademarks from descriptive terms by following the capitalization style used by the manufacturer.

SYBEX is not affiliated with any manufacturer.

Every effort has been made to supply complete and accurate information. However, SYBEX assumes no responsibility for its use, nor for any infringement of the intellectual property rights of third parties which would result from such use.

Library of Congress Card Number: 90-72066
ISBN: 0-89588-708-8

Manufactured in the United States of America
10 9 8 7 6 5 4 3 2 1

*T*o

Paula

ACKNOWLEDGMENTS

First and foremost, I'd like to thank Patrick Moffitt, of the training division of SCO, who originally suggested that I write this book and who has provided invaluable assistance throughout the writing.

Many other people at SCO helped, especially Chris Durham who acted as technical editor, Debbie Steiman-Cameron who kindly reviewed the programming chapters, and Joe DiLelio who kept my UUCP link to SCO going. Others who responded to electronic calls for help, whom I only know by their user-IDs, are davidw, jeffr, keithr, natei, nedh, paulz, philn, and stewarta. Any remaining errors are, of course, my own responsibility.

I'd like to thank David Kishler of CompuServe for access to the UNIX Forum, Inmac for supplying photographs, and Telebit and Microcom for technical information and photographs. Ward Christensen and Frank da Cruz helped with the information on XMODEM and Kermit respectively when I originally wrote the material for *Mastering Serial Communications*.

Finally, I'd like to thank everyone at SYBEX who helped to pull the whole project together.

CONTENTS AT A GLANCE

TABLE OF CONTENTS

xvi

INTRODUCTION

This book arose out of a request by the training department of The Santa Cruz Operation (SCO). They were designing a course on UNIX communications, and could not find a book that covered all the material for the course. They were familiar with my book *Mastering Serial Communications* (SYBEX, 1986), which deals mainly with IBM PC communications, and suggested that I write a similar book for UNIX.

LAYOUT OF THE BOOK

I have divided the book into four sections. **Part I** contains a general introduction to serial communications, including the physical connections, the way in which data are transmitted, hardware and software handshaking, modems, and communications protocols.

Part II covers UNIX communications from the point of view of the general UNIX user, and assumes a working knowledge of UNIX. In this part I describe UNIX *mail* and other utility programs provided by UNIX for communicating with other UNIX users and transferring files between UNIX machines.

Part III describes UNIX communications from the system administrator's point of view. It explains serial device drivers, how to set up and configure serial ports, and how to configure UUCP, the suite of programs provided for UNIX-to-UNIX communications.

Finally, in **Part IV** I describe how programmers can incorporate serial communications into their C programs for UNIX.

VERSIONS OF UNIX COVERED

There are many different varieties of UNIX available, and it would be impracticable to cover all the subtle differences between them. The descriptions in this book are based on SCO XENIX and SCO UNIX, and the Honey DanBer version of UUCP. The general principles should hold good for other versions of UNIX, although individual file and directory names and sometimes the layout of particular files may differ between systems.

STYLISTIC CONVENTIONS

The names of UNIX commands are printed in a different typeface than the rest of the text. The names of the various UUCP programs are shown in italic, as are descriptive "placeholder" names in command parameters. Where the formats of individual commands are shown, you should substitute the actual file name or other parameters for the descriptors shown in italics. Parameters shown in square brackets are optional. For example:

mail *[options] [machine!]user*

In this example *user* is the only non-optional parameter, and the simplest form of the command would be to substitute a real user name for *user* as follows:

mail peterg

The example also indicates that you can optionally precede the user name by a machine name, and that there are other options that you can add.

All numbers are decimal unless otherwise stated. Hexadecimal numbers are followed by the indication *Hex*.

PART ONE

Introduction to Communications

In Part I of this book I will describe the hardware and software aspects of serial communications. Chapter 1 describes the RS-232 interface and how the physical connections are made, and Chapter 2 explains standard communications parameters such as baud rate and parity, and how data are transmitted serially. Chapter 3 explains handshaking, and Chapter 4 explains how modems work, and common commands used to control them. Chapter 5 explains the options available for telephone communications and introduces packet-switching networks. Chapter 6 describes different types of terminals and how they can be connected to a host computer. Finally, Chapter 7 describes the problems involved in transferring files between different systems, and some solutions.

1

Hardware
Interfacing

In order for two devices to be able to communicate, they must be connected in such a way that electrical signals transmitted by one are received by the other.

Communication can be achieved either directly, with wires connecting the two devices, or indirectly, with an intervening medium. This medium is most often the public telephone system, in which case *modems* (*m*odulator *dem*odulators) are used to convert the signals at one end into signals suitable for transmission along telephone wires, and to convert them back at the other end. Other media, such as fiber-optics cables and radio transmission, can also be used. The devices that enable the computers to communicate using these media are connected in much the same way as the more conventional serial devices; therefore, the principles described here for direct communication will apply for indirect communication as well.

This chapter discusses direct connection of two devices, including the cables and connectors required, and the commonly used standards that determine which wires are used for which purposes.

PLUGS AND SOCKETS

There are several different types of plugs and sockets for connecting cables to serial devices. The 25-pin and 9-pin *D-type connectors* (sometimes referred to as DB-25 and DB-9) are the most common, though there are other types in use, such as the circular DIN connectors used in some Apple computers. Some typical D-type connectors are shown in Figure 1.1.

D-type connectors (so named because face-on they are shaped somewhat like the letter D) contain a certain number of pins or sockets. Those with pins are male connectors and those with sockets are female connectors. Each pin or socket has a number, which is generally printed alongside on the connector. The pin connections on some common connectors are shown in Appendix A.

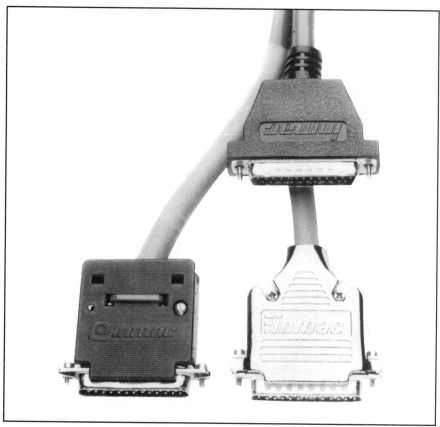

Figure 1.1: D-type connectors (photo courtesy of Inmac)

THE RS-232-C STANDARD

In order to make equipment from different manufacturers compatible, various standards have been designed. The most widely used is RS-232-C, published in 1969 by the Electronic Industries Association. The RS-232-C standard was originally drawn up to specify the connections between terminals and modems. It specifies the electrical characteristics of circuits between the two devices and gives names and numbers to the wires necessary for joining them. The circuit names allotted by RS-232-C (AA, AB, etc.) are hard to remember, and have been replaced in actual practice by abbreviations.

For example, line 2 is officially known as BA but more commonly as TXD (Transmitted Data). According to the RS-232-C standard, line 2 carries data from the terminal to the modem. For this to operate correctly, the terminal must produce output at line 2 and the modem must receive data on line 2. Therefore, line 2 is a transmitting line for some devices and a receiving line for others. A direct connection from line 2 on one device to line 2 on another device can be made only when one device transmits on line 2 and the other receives on line 2. Otherwise, both would be trying to transmit on the same line, and successful transmission of data would not be possible.

To prevent devices from attempting to talk to each other along the same lines, devices are divided into two types. Devices such as terminals, which use line 2 for output, are known as DTE (Data Terminal Equipment). Devices such as modems, which use line 2 for input, are known as DCE (Data Communication Equipment).

DTE AND DCE

According to RS-232-C, DTE devices should have male connectors and DCE devices should have female connectors. However, manufacturers do not always comply with this rule, so it is not always immediately obvious whether a given device is DTE or DCE.

When you know that one device is DTE and the other is DCE, you can, at least in theory, connect them easily by connecting line 2 to 2, 3 to 3, and so on. This is known as a straight connection. Because not all manufacturers comply with the standard, several problems can result. I will discuss these problems, and how to deal with the situation where both devices are DTE or both DCE, later in this chapter. For the time being, let's assume that one device is DTE and the other DCE, and that each is supplying the signals required by the other on the corresponding lines.

ONE-WAY COMMUNICATION

There are three main circuits that are used for communication: line 2 for data from DTE to DCE, line 3 for data from DCE to DTE, and line 7 for *signal ground*. Signal ground serves as a common reference point from which the polarity and voltage of the other lines can be determined. In the simplest case, where only one device transmits and one receives, only two lines need to be connected: line 2 or 3 and line 7. Figure 1.2 illustrates the simplest form of communication.

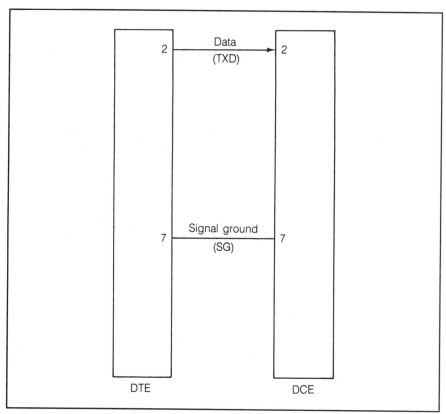

Figure 1.2: Simple one-way communication

HARDWARE HANDSHAKING

In many cases, it is necessary for the transmitting device to know whether the receiving device is ready to receive information. You might, for example, be sending data to a printer, and the speed of communication may be faster than the speed of the printer. The printer will have to be able to stop the computer from sending any more characters until it is ready to receive them. Similarly, you may be sending data from one computer to another, and the second computer cannot process the data as fast as it is coming in.

In both of these cases, information must be sent back from the receiving device to the transmitting device to indicate whether it is ready. This information is known as *flow control* or *handshaking*.

There are two types of handshaking: hardware and software. Both involve signals coming back from the receiving device to the transmitting device. With hardware handshaking, the receiving device sends a positive voltage along a dedicated handshaking circuit as long as it is ready to receive. When the transmitting computer receives a negative voltage, it knows to stop sending data. With software handshaking (which will be described in Chapter 3), the handshaking signals consist of special characters transmitted along the data circuits rather than along the handshaking circuits.

To incorporate hardware handshaking, at least one additional connection must be made to carry the signal. This brings the total number of lines to three: transmitted data, signal ground, and handshaking.

DTE TO DCE

When a DTE device is transmitting to a DCE device, line 2 is used for the data and line 7, as usual, carries the signal ground. A DCE device normally controls handshaking transmissions from a DTE device on line 6, known as DSR or Data Set Ready. If the printer is DCE and the computer DTE, line 6 on the printer should be connected to line 6 on the computer, and the printer will maintain a positive voltage on line 6 as long as it is able to receive data. When it wishes the computer to stop sending data, it will drop the voltage on line 6 to a negative state.

Often a second handshaking circuit, line 5, is also used by a DCE device to control transmissions from a DTE device. This circuit is called the CTS, or Clear To Send, line. Where two handshaking wires are used, the DTE device must be designed to transmit only when both lines are *high*, or positive. Sometimes the lines have different meanings. For example, one might tell the transmitting device to stop printing until a certain amount has been printed, and the other might indicate that the printer is out of paper. However, these meanings are not standardized. Since many computers are programmed not to transmit unless both handshaking lines are high, even printers that do not allocate a special meaning to the second line should at least maintain a positive voltage on it. Not all of them do, however, and sometimes the second signal must be faked by joining it to the first.

Figure 1.3 illustrates one-way communication from a DTE device to a DCE device with two handshaking wires.

DCE TO DTE

In order for a DCE device to talk to a DTE device, line 3 must be used for the data transmissions, and if handshaking is required, line 20 must be used to send handshaking from a DTE device to a DCE device. Line 20 is known as DTR or Data Terminal Ready. The secondary handshaking line, not always used, is line 4, Request to Send (RQS or RTS). Figure 1.4 illustrates DCE-to-DTE communications with handshaking.

TWO-WAY COMMUNICATIONS

Data are often transferred in two directions. This usually occurs when two computers communicate with each other, but also occurs in communicating between other devices when software handshaking is being used. The minimum number of lines necessary in two-way communication is three: transmitted data in each direction and signal ground. The addition of one handshaking line in each direction brings the total to five, as shown in Figure 1.5.

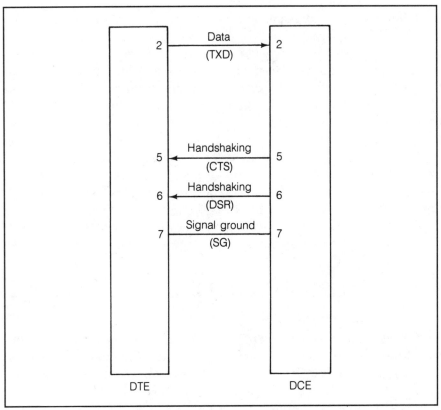

Figure 1.3: One-way communication with handshaking—DTE to DCE

When secondary handshaking lines are added in each direction, the total comes to seven. Two additional lines are often added to enable a modem to give more information to a computer or terminal. CD (Carrier Detect) is connected to pin 8, and is used to indicate the presence of a carrier signal. RI (Ring Indicator) is connected to pin 22, and indicates that the modem is being called by a remote device and would be ringing if it were a telephone. The total number of circuits now comes to nine, and these are shown in Figure 1.6. Although many other circuits are defined by RS-232-C, these nine are the most common and are the only ones normally connected to microcomputers. This is why some microcomputers use 9-pin connectors rather than the 25-pin type that would be necessary to carry the full set of RS-232-C circuits.

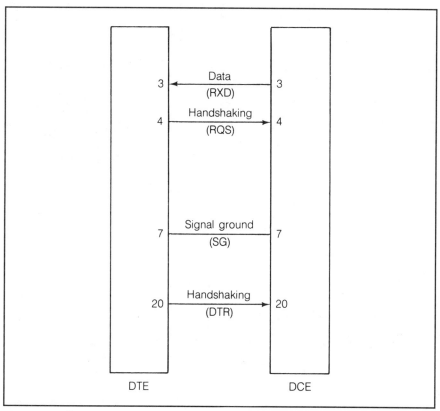

Figure 1.4: One-way communication with handshaking—DTE to DCE

NULL MODEMS

As I stated earlier, RS-232-C was originally devised to specify connections between terminals, which are DTE, and modems, which are DCE. However, it has been extended to apply to connections between many other kinds of devices that were not officially specified as being either DTE or DCE, such as microcomputers and printers.

Since there is no standard that indicates whether certain devices should be DTE or DCE, often you will have to connect two DTE devices or two DCE

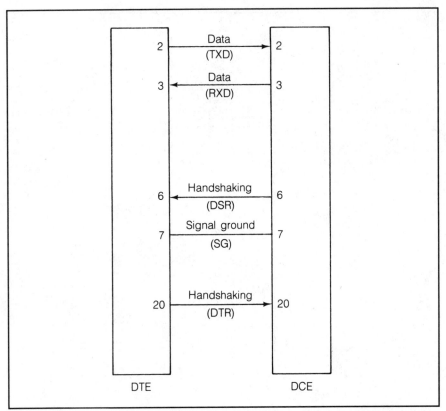

Figure 1.5: Two-way communication with main handshaking circuits

devices. In this case, you must connect line 2 on the first device to line 3 on the second, and line 3 on the first device to line 2 on the second. The handshaking wires must be crossed in the same way.

You can cross the wires either by connecting the devices with a cable in which the wires are crossed over, or by buying a special connector that connects both devices and performs the necessary crossing internally. In either case, the intervening cable or connector is called a *null modem*. It enables two DTE devices to talk to each other without the intervening DCE devices, or vice-versa. The wiring for a null modem is shown in Appendix A.

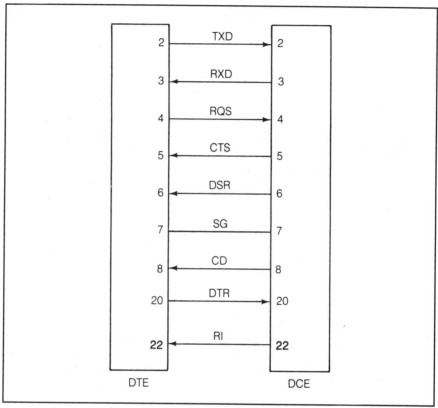

Figure 1.6: The nine standard RS-232 connections

ELECTRICAL SIGNALS

The RS-232-C standard lays down the characteristics of the electrical signals used in direct serial connections. There are only two states permitted: *SPACE*, corresponding to binary 0, where a positive voltage exists, and *MARK*, corresponding to binary 1, where a negative voltage exists.

On data lines (i.e., on lines 2 and 3), a positive voltage corresponds to a logical 0, and a negative voltage corresponds to a logical 1. On handshaking lines (e.g., DTR, DSR), a positive voltage indicates that the line is on, meaning "go ahead and send." A negative voltage means "stop."

Positive voltages (the SPACE state) are between +5 and +15 volts for outputs, and between +3 and +15 volts for inputs. The difference allows for voltage loss arising from cable length. Similarly, negative voltages (the MARK state) are specified as being between −5 and −15 volts for outputs, and between −3 and −15 volts for inputs.

Note that if too long a cable is used, the voltage levels fall outside the permitted boundaries. In addition, a buildup of capacitance affects the quality of the signal by smoothing out the transitions from positive to negative voltage. RS-232-C is not intended to be used for long distances, and 50 feet is generally considered the maximum distance using normal cable at usual transmission rates. If devices are too far apart, a modem or some other method of communication is necessary.

RS-449, 422-A, AND 423-A

A newer standard than RS-232-C, RS-449 tackles the same problems but allows for greater transmission speeds and a reduction in electrical crosstalk. RS-449 specifies a 37-pin connector and, in case that is not enough, offers an additional 9-pin connector. If you have soldered as many 25-pin plugs as I have (25 pins within the space of 1½ inches), you will not be overly enthusiastic about RS-449, which has not been widely adopted. RS-449 covers the mechanical specifications and circuit descriptions, but not the electrical characteristics. It is intended to be used in conjunction with RS-422-A and RS-423-A, which describe the electrical characteristics of balanced and unbalanced circuits respectively. Balanced circuits, used in higher-speed applications or where transmission problems are likely, use two wires, A and B. The MARK and SPACE conditions are signaled by changes in the polarity of the two wires by reference to each other, instead of a single wire changing in polarity by reference to a single common or signal ground.

Incidentally, the Electronic Industries Association (EIA) has been trying to encourage the use of the prefix EIA rather than RS for its standards. You will see the standards referred to both ways, but in this book I will refer to them by the better-known RS name.

INTERFACING RS-449 AND RS-232-C

It is possible to interconnect RS-449 and RS-232-C devices. The EIA addresses the procedure in its document entitled "Application Notes on Interconnection between Interface Circuits Using RS-449 and RS-232-C," or Industrial Electronics Bulletin No. 12. This document applies only to the RS-423 (unbalanced) circuits.

INTERFACING RS-232-C AND THE APPLE MACINTOSH

It is not theoretically possible to interface the Apple Macintosh with RS-232-C circuits, because RS-422, with which the Macintosh claims compliance, does not have a common signal ground by reference to which both the transmitted data line and the received data line vary. Nevertheless, the Macintosh has been designed in such a way as to make the interface possible. The ImageWriter printer often used with the Macintosh is a DTE RS-232-C device, and the cable used for connecting the Macintosh to the ImageWriter has a DB-25 connector, which can be used for interfacing to other serial devices. (Note that the Macintosh's *9-pin* DB connectors bear no relationship to the pin connections specified in RS-449.)

TROUBLESHOOTING

The following are some notes to help with problems you may encounter while connecting serial devices.

DO YOU NEED A NULL MODEM?

As I mentioned above, you need a null modem whenever you have to connect two devices that are both DTE or both DCE. In some cases, however, you may not know whether a device that you are trying to connect is DTE or whether it is DCE (newer devices such as mice and light pens often cause this problem). Since there is always the possibility that the two devices might be the same, you should try using a null modem connector if you cannot transmit with a straight connection.

HANDSHAKING PROBLEMS

If a printer does not respond to the transmitting device, it might be that the printer requires two handshaking lines to be high whereas the computer is providing only one. This is often the case with the IBM PC, which is capable of providing two lines but, unless specially programmed, provides only one. It is often possible to fake the second signal by connecting the subsidiary handshaking wire to the main one at the printer end of the cable.

If the microcomputer is not providing any handshaking signals at all, and the printer insists on receiving one or two, even more faking can be carried out by feeding the printer's own outgoing handshaking signal back into the printer as an incoming signal.

If a computer is not sending when it should be, it is probably because it is expecting a handshaking signal that it is not receiving. If a printer is setting only one handshaking line high, try connecting the other handshaking line to it at the computer end.

USING BREAK-OUT BOXES

If you do a lot of interfacing, I strongly recommend investing in a *break-out box*. This small device has two D-type connectors that can be inserted between two serial devices. Each line has a light, which is on when there is a signal on that circuit. The break-out box, therefore, allows you to see when data are being transmitted, and along which line, and also which handshaking lines are carrying a positive voltage. You can switch wires in and out and join wires by inserting jumpers into sockets.

By using a break-out box, you can experiment with changing connections without having to solder and desolder wire. Having established which connections are correct, you can then make up the appropriate cable. A typical break-out box is shown in Figure 1.7.

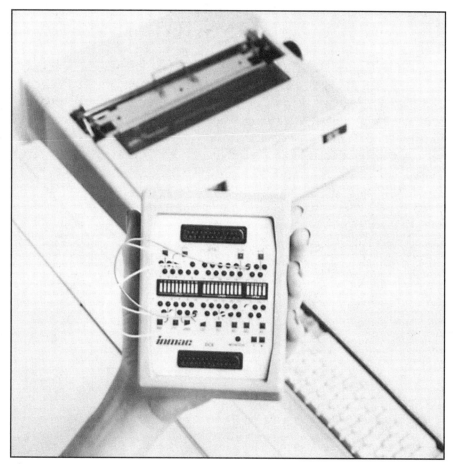

Figure 1.7: A break-out box (photo courtesy of Inmac)

OTHER PROBLEMS

If your receiving device is receiving garbage, the problem is probably one of character transmission. See Chapter 2 for more information.

For examples of interfacing various devices, as well as more information about RS-232, refer to Joe Campbell, *The RS-232 Solution*, second edition (SYBEX, 1989).

SUMMARY

In this chapter, I have described the main ways that serial devices can be connected. I have described the plugs and sockets, the main circuits, and the voltage levels. I have introduced the concept of hardware handshaking, and outlined some suggested problem-solving techniques. You may find after reading the book that you want to refer back to some of the reference material I have included on this subject. For easy reference I have placed some figures in Appendix A that illustrate the pin positions of a number of common connectors. In the next chapter, I will describe how data are converted into suitable form for transmission.

2

Character
Transmission

In the last chapter, we examined the hardware connections between two devices. In this chapter, we will look at how individual characters are encoded and sent along the wires. The principles discussed here apply both to signals sent along telephone wires between modems and to signals sent along cables between computers.

DATA FORMAT WITHIN THE COMPUTER

In order to understand the transmission of data, we must first understand how it is stored within the computer.

BITS AND BYTES

In decimal notation, there are ten digits—zero to nine. Adding a zero to the end multiplies a number by ten. In *binary notation*, there are only two digits—zero and one. Adding a zero to the end of a number multiplies the number by two.

Each binary digit of zero or one is known as a *bit*. Eight bits generally make up a *byte*. Accordingly, the values for a byte can range from 00000000 to 11111111, or 0 to 255 in decimal.

By convention the rightmost bit in a byte is referred to as *bit zero*. The leftmost bit is known as *bit seven*. Bit zero is also known as the *least significant bit*, and bit seven as the *most significant bit*. Figure 2.1 shows the number 35 in binary.

Almost all computers work in binary because it is easy to code zeros and ones as positive and negative voltages. In most computers, the smallest unit of storage that can be referred to by means of a memory address is the byte. Therefore, when information is stored and manipulated in a computer it is normally converted into a sequence of bytes.

Bit number	7	6	5	4	3	2	1	0
Value if set	128	64	32	16	8	4	2	1
Setting	0	0	1	0	0	0	1	1
Value as set	0	0	32	0	0	0	2	1

Figure 2.1: Number 35 in binary

CODING TEXT

When text (alphabetical characters, punctuation marks, etc.) is stored in a computer, each different character is represented by a different number. These numbers normally range from 0 through 127, or from 0 through 255. Since a byte can have a value from 0 through 255, it is natural to allocate one byte to each letter or punctuation mark in text data.

There are two different conventions for mapping characters to numbers: EBCDIC (Extended Binary Coded Decimal Interchange Code), which is used in IBM computers other than the IBM PC series, and ASCII (American Standard Code for Information Interchange), which is used in most other computers. We will be dealing only with the ASCII method in this book.

The official ASCII table gives numbers between 32 and 126 to the numerals, alphabetic characters, punctuation marks, and other common symbols. The numbers from 0 to 31 and 127 have special meanings such as carriage return, line feed, and other *nondisplayable characters.*

For example, uppercase A is stored as decimal 65; in binary this is 01000001. A comma is stored as decimal 44, which is 00101100 in binary.

Since the number 127 in binary uses only seven bits, all the characters represented by 0 through 127 can be stored in one byte, leaving one extra bit. Because we name the bits in a byte zero through seven, we can see that the ASCII code uses only bits zero through six. Bit seven is spare.

Many computers use the full eight bits of each byte for coding letters, giving a total of 256 different combinations. The first 128 follow the ASCII mapping, and the remainder are used for foreign characters, mathematical symbols, graphics characters, and so on, as the designer wishes. Unfortunately, there is no standard for these *extended characters,* which tend to have different meanings on different computers.

SPECIAL ASCII CHARACTERS

The first 32 codes in the ASCII table do not represent printable characters, but have special meanings, as listed in Table 2.1. Many of them were specifically designed to aid communications.

Table 2.1: The Special ASCII Codes

CODE	CHARACTER	DESCRIPTION
0	NULL	A method of deliberately causing a delay. It used to be necessary (because printers were so slow) to send nulls after each carriage return to allow the printer carriage to return to the left-hand edge of the page. It is also used for a variety of other purposes.
1	SOH	Start of heading. Indicates that the following text is part of a title
2	STX	Start of text. Indicates the start of the actual text of the message
3	ETX	End of text
4	EOT	End of transmission
5	ENQ	Enquiry. Normally used as part of a software handshaking sequence asking the receiving computer to acknowledge receipt of the message
6	ACK	Acknowledges receipt of a message
7	BEL	Rings the terminal bell or equivalent
8	BS	Backspace
9	HT	Horizontal tab
10	LF	Line feed. Causes a skip to the same position one line below

Table 2.1: The Special ASCII Codes (continued)

CODE	CHARACTER	DESCRIPTION
11	VT	Vertical tab
12	FF	Form feed. Advances to a new page
13	CR	Carriage return. Moves to the beginning of the line. Sometimes also causes a line feed, but this varies
14	SO	Shift out. Marks the start of a special control-code sequence. Esc is often used instead now (see below)
15	SI	Switch in. Marks the end of a control-code sequence initiated by SO
16	DLE	Data link escape. Similar to Esc
17	DC1	
18	DC2	Device control 1 to 4. Four spare codes to be used as desired; sometimes used in software handshaking
19	DC3	
20	DC4	
21	NAK	Negative acknowledgement. Indicates that a transmission was not received correctly. For example, a parity error may have been detected.
22	SYN	Synchronous idle. Similar to a NULL, but used in synchronous communication to keep two devices synchronized between transmission. Synchronous communications are described later in this chapter.
23	ETB	End of transmission block. Used where transmissions are divided into blocks for error-checking purposes
24	CAN	Cancel. Disregard the data sent
25	EM	End of medium. Indicates approaching end of a paper tape

Table 2.1: The Special ASCII Codes (continued)

CODE	CHARACTER	DESCRIPTION
26	SUB	Substitute. Corrects an erroneously sent character. Also used in practice to indicate end of transmission
27	Esc	Escape. Indicates the start of a sequence of characters with special meaning to the recipient
28	FS	
29	GS	File, Group, Record, and Unit separator, respectively. Mark boundaries between text segments
30	RS	
31	US	
127	DEL	Delete the preceding character

Codes 1 through 26 are also referred to as Ctrl-A through Ctrl-Z, and can normally be generated on a computer keyboard by holding down the key marked Ctrl and pressing the appropriate alphabetical key at the same time (thus, 1=Ctrl-A, 2=Ctrl-B, and so on). Some of the codes can also be achieved by pressing dedicated keys, such as Tab for code 9 or Return for code 13.

CODING NONTEXTUAL MATERIAL

Of course, not all the material stored in a computer is in text form. Program instructions, numeric data, and graphic images, for example, are not stored in ASCII form.

These types of data are normally coded in such a way as to use all 256 possible values of a byte. Numbers are stored in binary form and can extend over several bytes. Program instructions often consist of one or two bytes. We often refer to this type of material, in a communications context, as *binary data* (even though text is also stored in binary form).

Since the bytes holding nontextual data can be of any value, at times they will correspond to values that have special meanings in the ASCII table. This can cause complications if you are transmitting data and your receiving device happens to interpret a nontextual byte to mean the end of the message. In this case the data cannot be sent in their *raw* form, because a byte in the middle of the message might accidentally correspond to the end-of-message symbol, and the receiving device would stop listening.

Accordingly, certain protocols have been designed to cope with this problem; some are described in Chapter 7.

CONVERSION TO SERIAL FORM

Almost all computers store and manipulate their data in parallel. This means that when a byte is sent from one part of the computer to another it is not sent one bit at a time but several bits at a time over a number of wires running in parallel. The number of bits sent at a time varies from machine to machine, but is normally eight or a multiple of eight. Therefore, a computer can work with at least one byte and often two or more bytes at once.

Since communication from a computer to many other devices is done serially, meaning that data are sent one bit at a time, a communication interface must be able to take bytes that are received in parallel, and send out the individual bits separately.

As we have seen, the data lines in serial communications can only be in either MARK or SPACE condition, which in direct connection equates to negative or positive voltages, respectively. Any transmitted data must first be translated into a sequence of MARKs and SPACEs. For the purposes of this translation, a MARK represents a one, and a SPACE represents a zero.

SYNCHRONOUS AND ASYNCHRONOUS COMMUNICATIONS

Once the data are converted to serial form, there are two ways that they can be communicated: *synchronously* or *asynchronously*.

When data are being transmitted by someone typing at a keyboard, they are almost always sent and received asynchronously. A person typing at a keyboard cannot type at a continuous, even pace; therefore, when the computer receives the letters, there are differing gaps between each character. If the individual letters are being serially transmitted as they are typed, the irregular gaps between the characters make it impossible for a receiving device, after receiving one character, to tell exactly when the next one will arrive. Because of this lack of continuity, it is necessary to place extra bits before and after each character to indicate to the receiving device the beginning and end of the character. These extra bits are known as *start bits* and *stop bits*. In addition, another bit, known as the *parity bit*, is often added to enable errors to be detected (described below). This method is known as *asynchronous communication*.

When characters are sent in a block at machine speed, they can be spaced out regularly. It is no longer necessary for each character to have start and stop bits, because once the first character has been received the receiving device can predict exactly when the following characters will arrive. In other words, it can synchronize itself with the transmitting computer. This method is known as *synchronous communication*.

Because asynchronous communication requires start and stop bits to be added to each character, it can take about 20 percent longer to transmit a file compared with synchronous communication. This difference is not noticeable when the source of the transmission is a human typing at a terminal, since the limiting speed factor there is how fast the person can type rather than how fast the characters can be transmitted.

Outside of the IBM mainframe world, where synchronous terminals are commonly used, most serial communication takes place asynchronously. This applies to almost all communication between microcomputers, terminals, and UNIX systems. For this reason, the remainder of this chapter will concentrate on asynchronous communications.

FRAMING

In the case of asynchronous serial communications, the bits representing one byte, which are known as the *data bits*, are preceded and followed by start, stop, and parity bits, which are described fully in this section. This process is known as *framing*.

The number of bits representing one character varies according to the communications protocol in use. The number used describes the number of data bits, or the *word length*. It is normally either seven or eight bits. Each character is sent in a group consisting of a start bit, the character (data bits), an optional parity bit, and one or more stop bits. For the sake of clarity, I will refer to each group consisting of one character and its associated bits as a *frame*, in order to avoid the confusion that can occur when the word *character* refers sometimes to the data bits and sometimes to the full group with start, stop, and parity bits. Two examples of transmitted frames are shown in Figure 2.2.

START BITS

A start bit is always added at the beginning of a frame to alert the receiving device that data are arriving and to synchronize the mechanism that separates out the individual bits. A start bit is a SPACE, or binary 0.

With direct connection, a SPACE or 0 is transmitted as a positive voltage. The voltage between frames is negative. Accordingly, at the start of each frame, the voltage changes from negative to positive.

DATA BITS

The serial communications standards, called *protocols*, allow for the transmission of different lengths of characters, or words. When communications software asks you to select word length, it is asking whether you want to send seven-bit characters or eight-bit characters (sometimes other lengths are used, but this is rare). If all the data to be transmitted are in ASCII form, seven-bit words are sufficient. Remember that the ASCII table only assigns numbers from 0 to 127, all of which can be represented in seven bits.

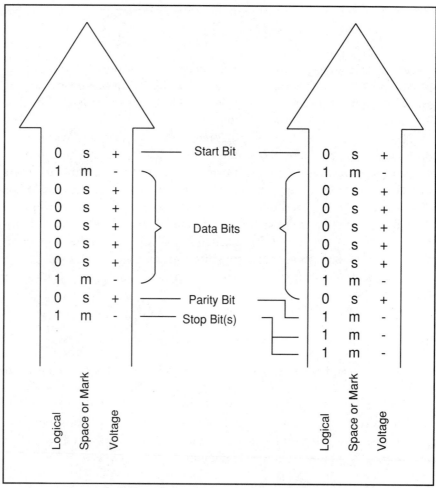

Figure 2.2: Two examples of transmitting the letter A

If non-ASCII data are to be transmitted (for example, text using extended character sets or binary data), all eight bits of each byte are needed, and you cannot use a seven-bit protocol unless the data are first converted into seven-bit format. This is discussed more fully in Chapter 7.

Data bits are transmitted with the least significant bit—that is, bit zero—first. If you were to write or type the data normally, your last stroke would be the first transmitted. Thus the letter C, which is ASCII 67 decimal, would normally be printed as 01000011 in binary, but is transmitted 11000010 (or 1100001 as seven bits).

PARITY BIT

Parity checking is a method of testing whether the transmission is being received correctly. The sending device adds a parity bit, the value of which (0 or 1) depends on the contents of the data bits. The receiving device checks that the parity bit does indeed bear the correct relationship to the other bits. If it does not, something must have gone wrong during the transmission. Parity can be computed in any of the ways discussed below.

Even Parity

Even parity means that the number of marked data bits and the value of the parity bit add up to an even number. For example, the letter A in binary is 01000001. When you count the number of marked bits you get 2— an even number. For even parity, the total of the marked data and parity bits must be even, so the sending device sets the parity bit to 0. If the letter A is received with the parity bit set to 1, an error must have occurred during transmission.

Odd Parity

Odd parity means that the total number of marked data bits plus the value of the parity bit yields an odd number. So, again using the letter A, the parity bit would have to be set to 1, to bring the total of the bits to 3—an odd number.

No Parity

No parity means that there is no parity bit. A parity bit is not always used, and it is often ignored by the receiving device even when it is used. It all depends on how the two devices have been programmed.

SPACE Parity

Sometimes a parity bit will be used, but always set to 0. It is thus called *SPACE, or zero, parity.* This provides some error checking, since with seriously garbled transmissions the parity bit would sometimes be set to 1 indicating an error of some sort. SPACE parity can also be used to transmit seven-bit characters to a device that is expecting eight-bit characters. The receiving device interprets the parity bit as the last bit of the data word. If all the characters sent are standard ASCII characters, the eighth bit is never used anyway, so a 0 in that position is inconsequential. SPACE parity is sometimes referred to as *bit trimming.*

MARK Parity

MARK parity works the same way as SPACE parity except that the parity bit is always set to 1. Because a 1 in that position could be interpreted as adding to the value of the number, the device or the receiving computer must be programmed to ignore it. Mark parity is sometimes referred to as *bit forcing.*

STOP BITS

At the end of each frame, stop bits are sent. There can be one, one and a half, or two stop bits. There is always at least one stop bit. This ensures that there is a negative voltage for at least some period of time before the next frame so that the next frame can be recognized by its positive start bit. More than one stop bit is generally used when the receiving device requires extra time before it can handle the next incoming character.

One and a half bits means that the length of the bit is greater than that of a normal bit. The stop bits force a certain minimum "gap" between frames. They are sent as binary 1s, which, in direct connection, equal a negative voltage.

Two stop bits are usually used at 110 baud, which is the lowest transmission rate in general use. This is consistent with the requirements of older teletypewriter terminals, which use a low baud rate and require extra time to process characters.

BREAK

As explained previously when explaining start bits, between characters the data line is normally in MARK condition (negative voltage, binary 1). If a character consisted of all 0s, with eight data bits, and even parity, a SPACE or zero condition would exist for ten bits: the start bit, the eight data bits, and the parity bit. This maximum SPACE condition would end when it reached the stop bit, which is negative. Thus, at the rate of 150 bits per second, a typical SPACE condition would last no more than $\frac{1}{15}$ of a second, or 66.67 milliseconds.

A longer SPACE condition than this, normally 100 to 600 milliseconds, is used as a special signal known as a *break*. The break is sometimes used as the mainframe's equivalent of Ctrl-C on Berkeley UNIX, or Del on System V UNIX. It interrupts whatever program is currently running and returns the user to the operating system, or to some earlier level of a menu hierarchy within a program. Like Ctrl-C or Del, it is useful for getting out of a program that has gone into an endless loop.

BAUD RATE

The baud rate expresses the number of discrete signals in one second. It is named for the French communications pioneer Baudot. In a binary transmission, it is the same as *bits per second* (bps), the number of *binary digits* transmitted in one second. There is a difference between the two, but they are often confused. Probably 200,000 people would tell you they have 1200-baud modems, and not one of them actually does! They are actually 1200 bps modems.

In direct RS-232 connections, a signal is in one of two states at any one time and the baud rate and the bps rate are the same. However, as we will see in Chapter 4, when a signal is transferred between modems it can be in one of several states. The signal length may be $\frac{1}{600}$ seconds (600 baud) but, since more than two bits of information can be transmitted with each change of state, the bps rate will be higher than the baud rate.

It is important to note that both baud rate and bps refer to the rate at which the bits within a single frame are transmitted. The gaps between the frames can be of variable length, usually because the characters are being keyed in at a variety of speeds. Accordingly, neither baud rate nor bps refers to the rate at which information is actually being transferred.

When each new character is received, the receiving device is resynchronized. Therefore, a start bit is needed to signal the start of a new frame and to trigger whatever mechanism is used by the receiving device to read and interpret the bits that follow.

Bps rates are generally in the series 110, 150, 300, 600, 1200, 2400, 4800, 9600, and 19200. The most common rates for modem communications are 1200 and 2400. The 1200 rate is common for computer-to-printer communications, and 9600 is common for terminal-to-computer connections.

TROUBLESHOOTING

When two devices are set up to communicate with each other, they must each agree on baud rate, word length, number of stop bits, and parity. If you find that nothing at all is being received, the error probably lies in the physical connection: the data are being sent along the wrong line, there is a break in the line, or the correct handshaking signals are not being received. If garbage is being received, the error probably lies in one of the areas discussed below.

BAUD-RATE MISMATCH

If the two devices are set at different baud rates, the receiving device may attempt to interpret the data (unless it is programmed to report parity and framing errors). Typically, you will see that the number of received characters differs from the number sent.

PARITY ERROR

A *parity error,* strictly speaking, indicates that data have been damaged in transmission. However, it can also mean that the two devices have not been set to agree on parity (odd, even, or none) or on word length.

WORD-LENGTH MISMATCH

If eight-bit words are being sent and the receiving device is expecting seven-bit words, you may not notice any difference in text transmissions, because often only the first seven bits are significant anyway. Because bit zero is sent first and bit seven is not used in genuine ASCII transmissions, its omission is not necessarily important. However, the receiving device may try to interpret the extra bit as a parity bit and report an error. Accordingly, a parity error does not necessarily mean that the data have been damaged in transmission; it may indicate a word-length mismatch.

If seven-bit words are being sent, and the receiving device is expecting eight-bit words, the parity bit may be treated as the missing eighth bit. Since the parity bit is generally 1 for half the characters and 0 for the other half, you will often find that the receiving device will display extended characters, such as graphics characters, in place of half the characters received.

STOP BITS

There should be no problem if two stop bits are sent and only one is expected. The extra stop bit simply merges into the gap that is permitted between characters. However, sending one stop bit when two are required could cause a problem, depending on the characteristics of the receiving device. This is not likely to be a problem with modern equipment.

FRAMING ERROR

A *framing error* indicates a mismatch in the number of bits and is usually reported when an expected stop bit is not received.

3

Handshaking
and Buffers

Handshaking refers to methods with which a receiving device can control the flow of data from a transmitting device. Sometimes a printer cannot print characters as fast as it receives them from a sending computer. It must use handshaking to cause the computer to suspend transmission. Handshaking is also useful when the printer runs out of paper or when a computer sends data to another computer and the receiving computer cannot process the characters as fast as they are being received.

When you know that a receiving device can process received characters faster than the transmission rate, you can dispense with handshaking.

HARDWARE HANDSHAKING

Hardware handshaking, as discussed in Chapter 1, is the use of dedicated handshaking circuits to control the transmission of data. To summarize: DCE equipment normally uses DSR (Data Set Ready) as a main handshaking line to tell DTE that it is powered up and ready to control transmissions it is receiving. It can also use CTS (Clear to Send) as a subsidiary handshaking line. DTE equipment, on the other hand, uses DTR (Data Terminal Ready) as a main handshaking line to tell DCE that it is ready to receive, and RTS (Request to Send) as a subsidiary handshaking line. By convention, these handshaking wires carry a positive voltage when transmission is to be enabled, and a negative voltage when it is to be suspended. Note that many UNIX manufacturers will vary on their implementation of hardware handshaking.

For example, a serial printer configured as a DTE device will raise DTR to a positive voltage when it is ready to receive characters and lower it to a negative voltage when it wants to suspend the transmission. It can also use RTS as a subsidiary handshaking line. As explained in Chapter 1, if the computer is also a DTE device, a null modem must be used to transpose the signals. This means that DTR and RTS from the printer become DSR and CTS at the computer. Many computers are programmed not to transmit unless both DSR and CTS are high.

The flowchart in Figure 3.1 illustrates a typical sequence for a computer sending data to a printer using hardware handshaking.

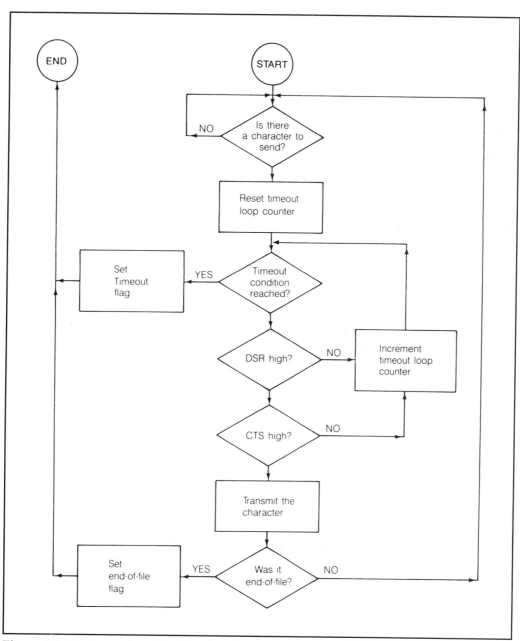

Figure 3.1: Hardware-handshaking flowchart for sending device

SOFTWARE HANDSHAKING

When handshaking signals are sent as data along the data wires (TXD and RXD, lines 2 and 3), instead of along dedicated handshaking circuits as in hardware handshaking, this is called *software handshaking*. This method is generally used where two computers are communicating (either directly or via a modem) and when two-way communication is possible.

Several standard protocols have been established to govern software handshaking, the most common of which is XON/XOFF.

XON/XOFF

Under this protocol, the receiving device sends ASCII character DC3 (19 decimal, 13H) to the transmitting device when it wants to stop the transmitting device from sending characters. It sends ASCII character DC1 (17 decimal, 11H) when it wants the transmissions to resume.

In normal practice, a *buffer* will be implemented. The DC3 character will be sent to the transmitter when the buffer is almost full and the DC1 character will be sent when the buffer is almost empty. (Buffers are described later in this chapter.)

The flowchart in Figure 3.2 illustrates a typical sequence for a computer sending data to a printer using XON/XOFF protocol.

ETX/ACK

In the end-of-transmission/acknowledge (ETX/ACK) method, data are sent in fixed-length batches. After sending each batch, the transmitting device sends an ETX (end of transmission) character, ASCII 3. The receiving device acknowledges receipt of the transmission by sending an ACK character, ASCII 6. Sometimes a NAK (negative acknowledge) character, ASCII 21, is sent back by the receiving device to indicate that errors were detected.

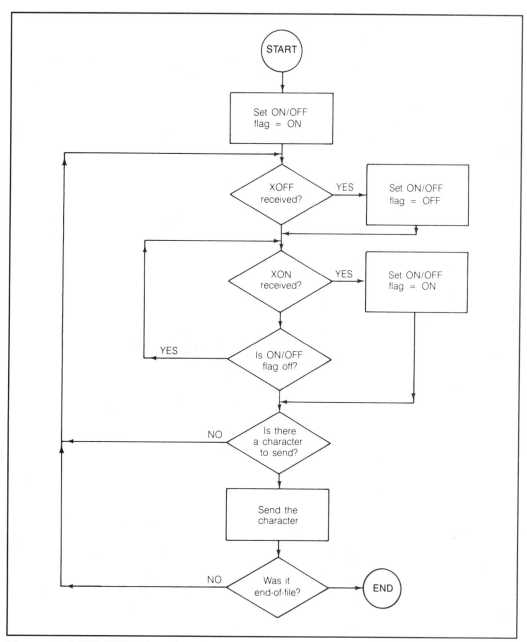

Figure 3.2: XON/XOFF flowchart for sending device

COMBINED HARDWARE AND SOFTWARE HANDSHAKING

Imagine that you are using a personal computer or a terminal to communicate with a mainframe computer via a modem. Your modem probably uses hardware handshaking with your computer. The mainframe's modem might be using hardware handshaking with the mainframe. But the mainframe uses software handshaking with your computer.

Accordingly, your computer must be programmed to communicate only when the DSR line from the modem is high (and possibly only if carrier detect, or CD, is high) and a software stop signal has not been received. This can complicate the flowchart. However, some computers take care of the hardware handshaking automatically, and wait for the hardware handshaking signals to be high before sending a character, so that your program need only deal with software handshaking.

BUFFERS

A *buffer* is an area of memory into which received characters or characters to be transmitted are placed. The use of a buffer reduces the number of handshaking signals that must be sent, because data can be transmitted in large blocks rather than character by character.

INPUT BUFFERS

An *input buffer* is used when the receiving device is receiving characters faster than it can deal with them. For example, a printer might be receiving characters at 1200 baud but only printing them at the equivalent of 300 baud. Rather than have the printer instruct the sending computer to stop after each character until it has been printed, the printer designer often sets aside an area of memory within the printer that has the capacity to store a given number of characters.

This area of memory is known as an *input buffer*. It is possible to think of this buffer as a water tank. The tank is being filled at the top, and at the same time it is being emptied at the bottom. A stop signal is sent when the buffer is almost full. The restart signal is sent when the buffer is almost empty. If the printer waited until the buffer was completely full before it said stop, and said start as soon as there was any room at all, the buffering would be defeated as soon as the buffer was filled for the first time. From then on it would be saying stop after each character was received and start after it had been processed, just as if there were no buffering at all.

Another reason for sending the stop signal before the buffer is completely full is to avoid losing characters that might be received simultaneously with the stop signal.

If hardware handshaking is in effect, a stop signal usually causes the sending device to suspend transmission immediately. With software handshaking, however, there is likely to be a time delay before the stop command takes effect, because the stop command has to be processed by the sending machine, and characters can be sent out concurrently with this processing.

The next three figures illustrate various stages in the filling and emptying of a printer buffer. Figure 3.3 shows the buffer half-full, at which

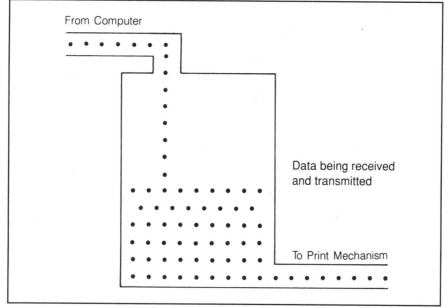

Figure 3.3: Buffer half-full

stage it is both receiving characters from the computer and sending characters to the printing mechanism. Figure 3.4 shows the buffer almost full, at which stage the printer asks the computer to stop sending data by lowering the handshaking lines or sending XOFF. Figure 3.5 shows an almost empty buffer; at this stage the printer orders the computer to resume sending characters by raising the handshaking lines or sending XON.

OUTPUT BUFFERS

An *output buffer* refers to an area into which data are placed prior to being transmitted. This reduces operator inconvenience. For example, imagine you are typing at the keyboard, and the characters you type are being sent directly to a printer or other device. When the printer has received all the information it can handle and sends a signal to stop, you actually have to stop typing. With buffered output, however, you can continue typing until you fill the output buffer, and by that time the printer

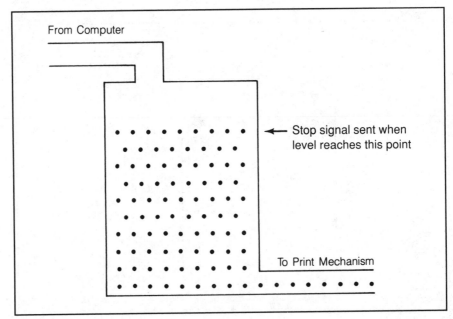

Figure 3.4: Buffer almost full

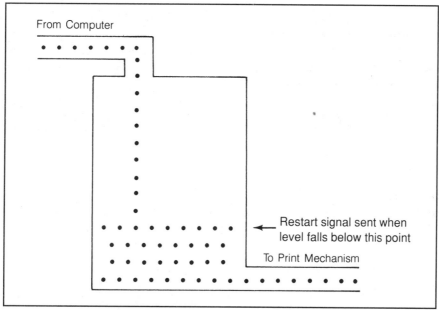

From Computer

Restart signal sent when
level falls below this point

To Print Mechanism

Figure 3.5: Buffer almost empy

will probably be ready to send a start signal again. In practice, most computers have a keyboard input buffer also, into which characters are placed as they are typed. Programs then take their input from the keyboard buffer.

IN-LINE BUFFERS

It is possible to purchase devices that stand between a computer and a printer and contain a large buffer. These *in-line buffers* receive characters from a computer and send them to a printer. They receive data much more quickly than a printer normally does, and can send them on to a printer at the appropriate baud rate for the printer.

From the point of view of the computer, it is just sending data to a very fast printer. From the point of view of the operator, the operation is complete as soon as the document has been sent to the buffer (assuming the document fits into the buffer), and he or she can continue creating a new document while the first one is still being printed out.

Some sophisticated in-line buffers can handle extra tasks such as conversion from serial to parallel, switching between printers, printing multiple copies of a document, and storing data received by a modem for subsequent processing by a computer.

4

Modems

A modem transforms data received from a computer in serial form into a form suitable for transmission through the telephone system, and vice versa. Modems can be used for transferring data between two computers at remote locations, or for connecting a terminal to a computer in circumstances where a direct connection is not possible.

We have already discussed how data are passed between two devices connected directly through a serial connection. Interposing two modems and a telephone wire does not affect the baud rate, the number of data bits, parity bits, stop bits, or software handshaking. What the modem does is convert the plus and minus voltages that represent the individual bits of each character into signals appropriate for telephone communications. Different modems work in different ways; the most popular types of modems are described in this chapter.

TYPES OF MODEMS

Connecting two computers, via modems, to the telephone system is by no means the whole story. As far as the user is concerned, the message disappears into the telephone system at one end and reappears out of it at the other end. Meanwhile, the signal may have passed through the cables of the originator's local telephone company to a long-distance telephone company, been bounced up to that company's satellite and back, and passed to the recipient via another local telephone company. In the case of communication with another person via CompuServe, all of the above may take place, with the additional intervention of two network operators (and maybe their satellites) and CompuServe's mainframe computers.

Fortunately for us, we can use one of the established protocols for modem communication discussed below and, in most cases, forget about the rest. Other protocols exist, but these are the ones in common use in the United States.

300-BPS MODEMS

When the plus and minus voltage signals are sent from the transmitting computer to a 300 bps modem, they are converted into tones. One tone is used to represent a positive voltage, and another to represent a negative voltage. In order for two-way communication to be possible, four different tones are used: two for the *originating* modem (the one that starts the communication) and two for the *answering* modem. The four tones used are defined in the Bell 103 standard, and are listed below:

- Originator transmits logic 0, positive voltage: 1070 Hz

- Originator transmits logic 1, negative voltage: 1270 Hz

- Answerer transmits logic 0, positive voltage: 2025 Hz

- Answerer transmits logic 1, negative voltage: 2225 Hz

This technique is known as *frequency shift keying,* or *FSK.*

1200-BPS MODEMS

Modems communicating at 1200 bps generally follow the Bell 212A system. (Note that modems that allow operation at 300 and 1200 bps actually include two modems, one following the Bell 103 standard and one following the 212A standard.) Instead of using four discrete tones to represent the individual bits, they use *phase modulation* techniques. A carrier signal is phase modulated in various ways to represent different combinations of bits.

A carrier signal can be in one of four different states, and can transmit two bits of information at once. For example, if we call the four states A, B, C, and D, state A could represent 00, state B 01, state C 10, and state D 11. Although technical factors limit to 600 per second the number of times the signal can change from one state to another, 1200 bits of information per second can be transmitted.

The four states are achieved by the use of four phase angles, and the technique is known as *phase shift keying,* or *PSK.* Two different carrier signals are used: the originator uses 1200 Hz and the answerer uses 2400 Hz.

2400-BPS MODEMS

In order to achieve a higher rate of information transmission, the number of carrier signal states can be increased again. Under the V.22 bis protocol, twelve phase angles and three amplitudes are used. This is known as *phase amplitude modulation*, or *PAM*.

PAM yields 36 different states, which can produce six bits of information at each change of state, compared with the two bits available under PSK as described above. This could theoretically result in 3600 bps (6 bits per state, 600 states per second), but the standard rate using this method is 2400 bps.

V.32 STANDARD 9600-BPS MODEMS

CCITT standard V.32 defines a standard for 9600-bps modems with the following features:

- QAM (quadrature amplitude modulation). This technique combines phase and amplitude modulation.

- Trellis encoding, which is a form of error detection and recovery.

- Full duplex operation, meaning that file transfers can take place in both directions at full speed, simultaneously.

This technology is expensive to implement, particularly because of the full-duplex requirement. Complex circuitry is needed to cancel out the echoes that are inherent in the public telephone system. The following is a partial list of modems that, at the date of writing, follow the V.32 standard:

- AT&T 2296A

- Hayes Ultra 96

- Microcom QX/V32c

- Telebit T2500

- UDS V.32

- USRobotics Courier V.32

OTHER HIGH-SPEED MODEMS

A number of companies have developed alternative proprietary techniques for achieving 9600 bps and higher speeds. These modems are usually cheaper than V.32 modems. However, they suffer from the disadvantage that if you want to use them at their highest speeds you must have the same modem at each end of the connection. They generally support standard protocols at lower speeds, however. This means that if you have, for example, a Telebit Trailblazer Plus attached to your host system, people can call in at high speed using their own Telebit modem or at 1200 or 2400 bps using any standard modem.

Some examples of non-V.32 high speed modems are:

- Hayes V-series Smartmodem 9600
- USRobotics Courier HST
- Microcom AX/9624c
- Telebit Trailblazer Plus

ERROR CONTROL
AND DATA COMPRESSION

It has long been possible for communications software to detect errors and request retransmission automatically. (Some of the techniques are discussed elsewhere in this book.) Other software techniques can reduce transmission time by the use of *data compression*. Data compression can be achieved in a number of ways. For example, a word-processing document might have a lot of spaces in it. A number of successive spaces could be replaced by a special code, which would be expanded back into spaces at the other end. This would reduce the number of characters that had to be transmitted, and therefore reduce the transmission time.

Error detection and data compression are now being built into the modems themselves. This can result in greater speed and efficiency of transmission. There are two standards in common use—the proprietary methods incorporated in the Hayes V-series modems, and the various

levels of MNP protocols developed by Microcom, Inc., but licensed to
several different manufacturers.

Although there are several "levels" of MNP, the commonly established one is *MNP-5*. MNP-5 has been quite widely accepted, and in some
cases you do not even need to have an MNP modem at each end; MNP-5
is sometimes incorporated into communications software so that it can be
used with non-MNP modems. The combination of MNP-5 with a 9600
V.32 modem can result in speeds of around 18,000 bps. Microcom also has
a proprietary version of MNP, MNP-9, that is even faster. Figure 4.1 shows
the Microcom QX/V.32c modem, which can achieve a throughput of up to
30,000 bps.

Figure 4.1: Microcom QX/V.32c modem, capable of up to 30,000 bps (photo
courtesy of Microcom, Inc.)

The following is a list of some high-speed modems that support
MNP-5:

- Microcom QX/V.32c (also supports MNP-9 for up to 30,000 bps)
- Microcom QX/329c (V.32, MNP-5)

- USRobotics Courier V.32

- USRobotics Courier HST

- Hayes ULTRA Smartmodem 9600

MODEM SUPPORT FOR
FILE-TRANSFER PROTOCOLS

A rather interesting technique has been developed by Telebit to improve the performance of its modems even further. Later in this book we will describe some file-transfer protocols such as XMODEM. Telebit has incorporated into some of its products support for certain protocols that speed up file transfers. For example, when you transmit data using XMODEM, your computer sends a block of data and then waits for the receiving computer to acknowledge receipt. No data are transmitted during this waiting period. What Telebit does is to "acknowledge" each block at the *transmitting* end immediately after the block has been sent, without waiting for the remote computer to acknowledge. The transmitting modem then sends the next block, but retains the first block in memory. That way, if the receiving modem detects errors in the first block, it can signal the transmitting modem to retransmit the block, without involving the computers at all. Currently, the Telebit Trailblazer Plus and T2500 modems support Kermit, XMODEM, YMODEM, and *UUCP* "G" protocols in this way. Figure 4.2 shows the Telebit Trailblazer Plus modem.

CONNECTING THE
MODEM TO YOUR COMPUTER

As far as your computer is concerned, an external modem is just another serial device. The normal wire connections are made for transmitted data, received data, signal ground, and handshaking. In addition, you can also connect Carrier Detect (CD), line 8, so the modem can let the computer know when a carrier signal is present; and Ring Indicator (RI),

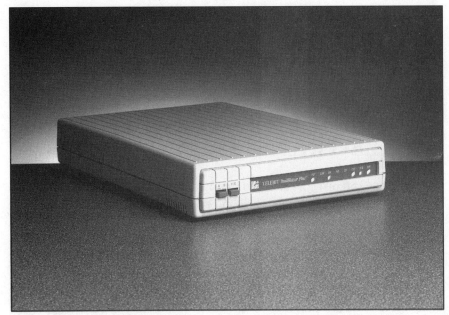

Figure 4.2: Telebit Trailblazer Plus modem, with internal support for file-transfer protocols (photo courtesy of Telebit Corporation)

line 22, so the modem can indicate that the telephone is ringing. A positive voltage on CD means that a carrier signal is present. A positive voltage on RI means that the telephone is ringing. Whether these signals are actually recognized by the computer depends on the communications software in use. Some modems send messages on the data line when the carrier is lost, in addition to lowering CD, and send messages when the telephone is ringing, in addition to raising RI.

In the case of an internal modem such as the Hayes Smartmodem 1200B, the modem is contained in a card that is plugged directly into the computer. The card appears to the computer to be a serial interface card, so that software does not need to know whether an internal or an external modem is in use. Other modems are external to the computer, and can be stand-alone modems such as those shown earlier in Figures 4.1 and 4.2, or rack-mounted such as those shown in Figure 4.3.

Note that hardware handshaking signals (DTR, DSR, etc.) are used to control communication between the computer and the modem. They are not passed along the line to the remote modem and computer. Accordingly,

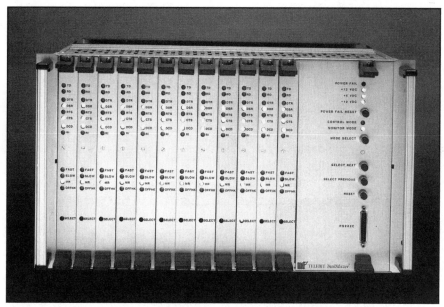

Figure 4.3: Rack-mounted modems (photo courtesy of Telebit Corporation)

to enable handshaking between the two computers, software handshaking must be used.

CONTROLLING THE MODEM

To use older types of modems, you have to dial the number using a conventional telephone, and then switch out the telephone and switch in the modem. Modern modems, on the other hand, usually do the dialing for you, and have many other built-in facilities that are discussed below.

Because the modems made by Hayes Microcomputer Products, Inc. have been so widely accepted by microcomputer users, the facilities and commands used by them have become a *de facto* standard in the industry. This has led competing modem manufacturers to follow suit, and many of them advertise their products as "Hayes compatible." The following information applies to the Hayes Smartmodem 1200 and 1200B modems, and should also apply to "Hayes compatible" modems if they are truly compatible.

COMMAND MODE AND ONLINE MODE

The modem is always in one of two states: local command state or online state. While the modem is in local command state, instructions can be given to it from the computer (in other words, through the serial interface between the computer and the modem). For example, these commands instruct the modem to dial a number, or to answer automatically when the telephone rings. The commands are diverted to the modem, and not transmitted.

Once connection is established with a remote modem, the local modem enters online state and no longer attempts to interpret the data being sent to it; instead, it transmits it. If the carrier signal is lost—for example, because the remote modem has hung up the phone—the modem will revert to local command state. It is possible to return from online to command state without disconnecting, by waiting for a guard time (the default is one second), typing an escape command (the default is +++), and waiting for one second before sending data to be interpreted as commands.

The instructions sent by the computer to the modem can be sent by communications software, or can be typed at the keyboard, provided the keyboard output can be redirected to the serial port. Instructions sent in command mode should be sent with seven data bits and one parity bit, or eight data bits and no parity bit. This can be accomplished easily in UNIX with the cu command. There should be one stop bit unless you are communicating at 110 bps, in which case there should be two stop bits. Hayes-compatible modems can detect rate automatically.

RESULT CODES

When the modem receives a command it returns a result code. This code can be in the form of either a text message or a numeric code. If you are controlling the modem through software, a numeric code is more appropriate. If you are controlling the modem from the keyboard, a text message is preferable. You can set the type of result code you want by using a command or by using switch settings. Table 4.1 shows the result codes.

Table 4.1: Hayes Modem Result Codes

DIGIT CODE	WORD CODE	MEANING
0	OK	Command executed
1	CONNECT	Connected at 0 –300 bps*
2	RING	Ringing signal detected
3	NO CARRIER	
4	ERROR	Error in command line
5	CONNECT 1200	Connected at 1200 bps*
6	NO DIALTONE	
7	BUSY	
8	NO ANSWER	
10	CONNECT 2400	Connected at 2400 bps

* With the 1200-bps modem, if X0 (the default) is set, result code 1 is given for both 0–300-bps and 1200-bps connections. This is to ensure compatibility with software written for 300-bps modems.

COMMAND LINES

Command lines all start with AT or at (not At or aT), unless otherwise specified. The modem can detect the baud rate, word length, and parity from these two characters. Of course, you must already have set up your computer for these parameters. Several commands can be given in one command line.

Dialing Commands

A comprehensive set of commands that tell the modem to dial numbers is provided with the manual accompanying the modems. Table 4.2 lists a summary of these commands.

Table 4.2: Hayes Modem Dialing Commands

COMMAND	MEANING
ATDT	Dial using Touch-Tones
ATDP	Dial using pulse tones
,	Pause between numbers each side of a comma
ATT	Use Touch-Tone as default
ATP	Use pulse as default
!	Transfer call
W	Wait for a second dial tone
@	Wait for one or more rings followed by five seconds of silence
O	(at end of command line) Return to online state
;	(at end of command line) Stay in command mode after executing command
R	Call an originate-only modem (see text)
/	Wait $\frac{1}{8}$ second

Following are some examples of how to use the dialing commands. Say you want to dial a number using Touch-Tone. Type the following:

    ATDT1234567

To dial a number using pulse tones, type

    ATDP1234567

After either of the above examples is typed, the modem dials the number and waits for a carrier signal. If it doesn't receive the carrier signal during a given time (the default is 30 seconds), it hangs up and returns a NO CARRIER result code.

If you need to dial 9 to get an outside line before you dial the number, type the following (the comma indicates a pause):

    ATDT9,1234567

To dial 9 for an outside line using Touch-Tone, then pause, and then dial the number using pulse dialing, enter

    ATDT9,P1234567

To dial 9 for an outside line, then pause, then dial a number, then pause again, and then transfer it to another number using #7, type

    ATDT9,1234567,!#71234

To dial an MCI or Sprint number, then wait for a second dial tone, and then dial another number, type the following (the spaces do not do anything but are included for clarity):

    ATDT 123 1234 W 123 123 1234

To call an originate-only modem, you must type R at the end of a dialing command line. You will recall that, by convention, the originating and answering modems use different frequencies. Typing *R* causes the modem to use answering frequencies even though it is originating the call.

    ATDT 123 1234R

ATX Commands

Although the term "Hayes compatible" is often used, there is actually no absolute standard since not even all Hayes modems work the same way. The newest Hayes modems have facilities such as the ability to report connection at different baud rates, detect the busy signal, and detect the dial tone. Since older software does not recognize the result codes returned by these new facilities, the default mode of the newer modems is to not use them. The new codes have to be enabled specifically with the ATX commands. The idea is that newer software that can handle the newer codes will issue the ATX command indicating which codes it can deal with.

The 300-bps models send the string "CONNECT" or numeric code 1. The 1200 and 2400-bps modems send CONNECT 1200 or CONNECT 2400 (numeric codes 5 or 10) as appropriate. Software that was written for the older modems might not recognize these new codes. Accordingly, if ATX0

is issued or if no ATX command is issued at all, the modem will return the
same code as a 300-bps modem. If any of the ATX1 through ATX4 commands are issued, the modem will return a connect code appropriate to
the bps rate. In addition, command ATX2 enables the NO DIALTONE
result code, ATX3 enables the BUSY result code, and ATX4 enables both
the NO DIALTONE and the BUSY result codes. The ATX commands are
summarized in Table 4.3.

Table 4.3: Hayes Modem ATX Codes

ATX NUMBER	CODE FOR 1200 BPS	WAIT FOR DIAL TONE	ERROR IF NO DIAL TONE	ERROR IF BUSY
0	1	No	No	No
1	5	No	No	No
2	5	Yes	Yes	No
3	5	No	No	Yes
4	5	Yes	Yes	Yes

Other Commands

There are quite a few remaining commands listed in Table 4.4. Most
are self-explanatory. You will see that the ATS0 through ATS16 commands
refer to setting modem registers. These registers record various
parameters such as timing. You can set a value into a register by issuing

Table 4.4: Other Hayes Modem Commands

COMMAND	MEANING
ATH	Hang up
ATZ	Hang up and reset to default settings
A/	Repeat last command
ATB0	Use international protocol

Table 4.4: Other Hayes Modem Commands (continued)

COMMAND	MEANING
ATB1	Revert to bell mode
ATC0	Turn off carrier signal
ATC1	Turn on carrier signal
ATE0	Turn off echo to screen
ATE1	Turn on echo to screen
ATF0	Turn off half-duplex
ATF1	Turn on half-duplex
ATL1–3	Set speaker volume
ATM0	Turn off speaker
ATM1	Turn on speaker until connected
ATM2	Turn on speaker and leave it on
ATQ0	Turn on result codes (the default)
ATQ1	Turn off result codes
ATV0	Display result codes as digits
ATV1	Display result codes as words
ATY1	Send four seconds of break signal before disconnecting. Disconnect if 1.6 seconds of break signal is received
ATY0	Neither send nor respond to break signals (the default)
ATH1	Operate the telephone line relay and auxiliary relay
ATH2	Operate the line relay
ATS0–16	Set the modem registers

the command ATS followed by the register number and the value. You can find out what the current contents of a register are by using ATS followed by the register number and a question mark. Table 4.5 shows the commonly used registers.

Table 4.5: Commonly Used Hayes Modem Registers

REGISTER	RANGE/UNITS	DESCRIPTION
S0	0–255 rings	Ring on which to answer
S6	2–255 seconds	Wait time for dial tone
S7	1– 60 seconds	Wait time for carrier
S13	bitmapped	UART status register

Answer Mode

The modem can be set to answer the telephone automatically. You can regulate the amount of times the phone rings before the modem answers by setting register S0. For example, if you want the modem to answer on the fifth ring, type

    ATS0=5

The default is S0=0, which tells the modem not to answer. There is a switch that can make the default S0=1, which means it will answer on the first ring unless instructed otherwise.

When the modem answers the telephone, it sends a carrier signal and waits for a response. If no carrier signal is received within the time set in register S7, it hangs up.

Detection of incoming baud rate is automatic, and the modem returns a result code indicating the baud rate. Your computer has to recognize this result code and adjust its own baud rate in order to respond to different incoming baud rates automatically.

PROGRAMMING THE MODEM

Commands sent to a modem can be entered at the keyboard or sent from a program. The modem, of course, cannot tell the difference. If you are using a program, you should probably turn off the text reporting of result codes, so that instead of reporting the results to you, the modem reports directly to the program which, in turn, interprets the codes itself.

Next, you should read the contents of all the registers and save them. This way, you will be able to restore the modem to the state it was in before the program started.

You can see that the powerful commands built into the modem make completely unattended operation possible. You can write programs that tell the modem to dial a particular number in the middle of the night, upload and download data, and so on. This allows businesses to take advantage of cheaper communication rates at off-peak hours, and a company can have all its branches dial in automatically with the day's figures every night, or exchange electronic mail, completely automatically.

5

Telecommunications
Methods

Most of us think of telecommunications in terms of picking up a telephone and dialing a number. The computer equivalent of this, using an auto-dial modem on one end and an auto-answer modem on the other, is the simplest method. There are, however, many other alternatives, and I will review some of these methods in this chapter.

DIRECT-DIALED CIRCUITS

The simplest way of communicating long-distance between computers is to hook up a conventional modem and dial the number of the remote computer which has been set up to answer the call automatically. This is known as direct dialing. In the United States, your call passes through the local telephone company, a long-distance carrier, and the local telephone company operating where the destination computer is located. You can choose your long-distance carrier from any of those available today, although the largest and most popular is still AT&T Communications. In most countries other than the United States, the call is handled by a single carrier—normally a public utility controlled by the government.

WATS (Wide Area Telephone Service) is a method of purchasing connect time in bulk. You pay a predetermined amount for unlimited use of a line for a given time period over a given distance. The arrangement can apply both to inbound calls, generally via toll-free 800 numbers, and to outbound calls.

Despite their simplicity and directness, there are a number of problems with the direct-dialed circuits. First, the cost of the call is often higher than with other methods. Second, the quality of the line is often insufficient for error-free communication. Third, very high-speed communications cannot be achieved over regular circuits.

LEASED LINES

When a large number of calls are made to one number, it can be worth installing a *leased line*. This is often done when, for example, a company's branch offices require constant access to a central computer. With leased lines, often called *point-to-point* connections; the customers don't need to dial. They simply pick up the phone and are automatically connected to the central computer. The customer generally has exclusive use of a particular circuit, although recently *virtual leased lines* have been introduced. With this type of line, one shares the physical circuits with other customers, but any one customer still has the impression of exclusivity. Leased lines can be either voice-grade or digital circuits.

VOICE GRADE

Voice-grade lines are designed primarily for voice communication, but can also be used for computer communications via modem. The quality of a leased line connection depends on several factors. Most local telephone circuits, between the user and the local telephone company, consist of two wires. These wires carry communications in both directions. Four wires are necessary for longer distances because amplification is required, and a two-wire circuit working in two directions at once cannot be amplified without first being converted into a four-wire circuit.

As we saw in Chapter 4, modern modems are capable of operating in both directions at the same time on a two-wire circuit because different frequencies are assigned to the orginator and the answerer. However, some modems are designed for use over leased lines and private circuits. These modems can take advantage of a four-wire connection by using each pair of wires in one direction only. In order for this to happen, a four-wire connection with the local telephone company must be installed. Accordingly, you may come across both two and four-wire leased lines.

Regular telephone circuits, as we all know, are susceptible to noisy lines. This noise disrupts data communications, because the modems sometimes interpret it as signals. It is possible, for an extra cost, to arrange for a higher than normal quality of line. This service is known as *conditioning*, and is provided by the long-distance carriers. AT&T, for example, offers several different levels of conditioning. With each higher level of conditioning the percentage of errors goes down and the cost goes up. Conditioning is achieved by using higher quality circuits and by the use of electronic methods of filtering out noise and increasing the strength of the signal.

DIGITAL CIRCUITS

If your communication requires higher speed or multiple circuits, a private digital circuit can be installed. These circuits transfer digital data synchronously at up to 56,000 bits per second. With digital circuits, modems are unnecessary, because the data are in digital form throughout the transmissions. Each circuit can carry a number of concurrent logical connections—in other words, it can carry several transmissions at the same time.

A digital system can be installed in such a way as to appear transparent to the user and even to the applications programmer. The terminals in an office can be connected to a *multiplexer,* which appears to the terminals just like the mainframe computer itself, regardless of the fact that the mainframe could actually be located on the other side of the continent. The multiplexer then communicates, via a high-speed digital line and a communications controller, with the mainframe computer. This technique is sometimes referred to as *multipoint* or *multidrop*. It is illustrated in Figure 5.1.

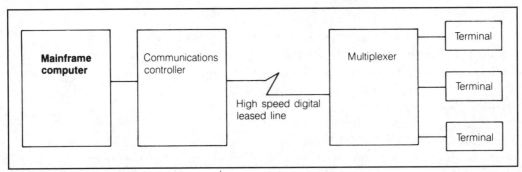

Figure 5.1: A multipoint connection

PACKET-SWITCHING NETWORKS

Value-added network operators such as Telenet and Tymnet (pronounced *time-net*) offer a service to people with long-distance computer communications requirements that aren't extensive enough to justify the installation of expensive equipment and circuitry. These less expensive networks allow a user to access a remote database, for example, by dialing up the local *node*, or access point, of a value-added network. The network then completes the connection to the remote computer. This is not only cheaper than making a long-distance telephone call directly to the remote computer, but also results in a better quality connection because the network circuits are optimized for computer, rather than voice, communications.

A major difference between the services provided by a long-distance carrier for telephone communications and value-added networks is that the destination computer is charged for the service, rather than the originating computer. The charges are, of course, passed back to the subscriber when an information source is being accessed.

These networks are called *packet-switching networks* because they use a method called packet switching to transmit messages. Packet switching involves dividing a message into individual packets, and delivering the packets to an addressee that reassembles them into the original message. Equipment for assembling and disassembling packets is known as a *PAD* (packet assembler/disassembler).

The packet-switching networks use high-speed digital links, which can be land lines or satellite communications. They use synchronous communications, usually with the X.25 protocol. The routes are continually being optimized, and successive packets of the same message need not necessarily follow the same path.

Each packet consists of some sort of header, the body of the message, an error-checking code, and an end-of-packet indicator. Packets are not all of the same length, and can sometimes consist of just a single character if data are being received slowly. The PAD can be instructed to wait for a certain number of characters before transmitting a packet, or to wait for a fixed length of time. The method chosen is important, since sometimes a per-packet charge is made. If a block of data is to be sent, clearly it would be advantageous for it to be sent in a single packet rather than as sequence of packets each of one character.

Connection with the packet-switching networks is normally made through regular dialed circuits, but direct connections can also be established. The packets can be constructed by the user or by the local node. Sometimes a charge is made for packet construction.

Despite the complexity of packet switching, you do not need to know any details about how the system works if you want to communicate with an information provider or utility such as CompuServe or Dialog via a network such as Tymnet. Just dial the local node using a regular asynchronous modem. You will then be asked to enter a terminal identifier code and a code for the host computer you wish to access. You may think that you are directly connected to the remote computer, but the echoing of characters is normally done by the local network. Otherwise, the communication would take much longer, because the time delay for characters to be sent to the remote computer and back can be considerable, especially if the network is using satellite links. Figure 5.2 illustrates the use of Tymnet to access CompuServe.

Packet switching is internally more complicated than direct dialing, but because of its lower costs and better quality connections, it is very popular. The fact that over half a million people regularly use the networks to access information providers such as CompuServe, Dow Jones News/Retrieval, and Dialog is testimony to their effectiveness and ease of use.

The following is a list of some major packet-switching networks:

- Internet, a U.S. government network

- Net 1000, the AT&T network

- Telenet, operated by GTE

- Tymnet, operated by BT Tymnet

- Uninet, operated by United Telecommunications and Control Data Corporation

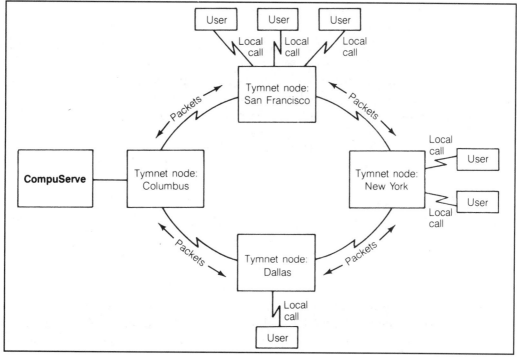

Figure 5.2: A multipoint connection

ISDN

A standard that is now being adopted, known as ISDN (Integrated Services Digital Network), promises to simplify digital communication of various types, including data, voice, and video. With ISDN, a single connection can carry several communications channels simultaneously.

BASIC RATE INTERFACE

There are two types of ISDN package. The first, known as the Basic Rate Interface (BRI), carries a pair of 64-kilobit-per-second digital channels and one 16-kilobit-per-second control channel. Each of the digital channels can be connected to up to eight serial devices such as personal computers, terminals, and fax machines. The time may come when the average household has the capability to send and receive faxes *and* to carry a voice communication and three or four computer sessions all simultaneously over a single telephone connection. This has considerable implications for the growing community of people who work from home, but it also gives rise to some fascinating possibilities for the future. The following are just a few of the possibilities:

- **voting**   People could vote without leaving their homes. Referenda might be held frequently and efficiently on important issues.

- **interactive television**   Game shows and other types of programs could use ISDN in a way already supported by some cable television systems.

- **alarm systems**   The digital channels could be used to carry signals indicating emergencies.

- **equipment servicing**   Some types of domestic equipment could be connected to a digital channel so that a remote service company could diagnose problems and perhaps even fix them. You might eventually be able to plug your car into a digital channel and have it tuned electronically.

- **medical monitoring**   Patients at home could be monitored electronically from a central location.

PRIMARY RATE INTERFACE

The second ISDN package, known as Primary Rate Interface (PRI), carries twenty-three 64-kilobit-per-second digital channels and one 64-kilobit-per-second control channel. This package is designed for businesses that have far more extensive communications needs. Digital channels can be combined to achieve higher throughput where necessary so that high-speed data communications or video can be carried.

6

Terminal-to-Host
Communications

In this chapter I will describe the various types of terminals and ways in which microcomputers can be used as terminals.

Most communication between humans and computers is through terminals. Terminals vary widely in their characteristics, but they are all primarily intended to take data entered at a keyboard or other human input device and transmit it to the host computer.

DUMB TERMINALS

Dumb terminals are terminals that depend on the host computer for all operations and do not do any processing of data on their own.

TELETYPE TERMINALS

The most basic type of terminal is the Teletype, which consists of a keyboard, printer, and punched tape device. Punched tapes can be created in local mode, edited if you are clever enough to know which holes to change, and fed back in to be read by the machine and transmitted to the host computer. Teletypes are practically obsolete now, but their influence remains, since their characteristics form the lowest common denominator to which many programs, especially operating system utilities, still conform. Many of these programs make no attempt to present attractive screens, since until recently you could not assume that the user had a screen at all.

VIDEO TERMINALS IN TELETYPE MODE

The next most basic device is a terminal that has a screen, but no full-screen processing. In other words, the text is displayed one line at a time, with the existing text scrolling up when the bottom of the screen is reached. This is known as *Teletype mode,* and basically treats the screen as a printer. PC-DOS works in this way, as do most information services. This enables them to be accessible from as many types of terminals as possible.

FULL-SCREEN PROCESSING

The most advanced of the dumb terminals use *full-screen processing*. With full-screen processing, data can be presented at different places on the screen, rather than as a sequence of lines. The terminal has sufficient memory to store all the characters currently displayed (typically 24 or 25 lines of 80 columns) and their *attributes* (inverse, underline, blinking, intensity, and character set). By using special sequences of characters you can clear the screen, move the cursor to a position on the screen, select an attribute, and so on. These sequences are known as *escape sequences* because they generally start with the escape character (27 decimal, 1B hex).

Unfortunately, different terminals use different escape sequences to achieve similar results. This means that software that is to be used on different terminals has to be configurable with the characteristics of the terminal in use at any one time. Most dumb terminals, however, conform to one of a small group of standards such as DEC VT100 or Lear-Siegler ADM3A. That is, they are either standard models produced by a major manufacturer or emulations of one of the major models.

INTELLIGENT TERMINALS

Intelligent terminals are so called because they are capable of processing information on their own. With the advent of cheap microprocessors it became logical to incorporate them into terminals. Many of the standard data-entry tasks require very little computing power, so it saves time and resources to handle these simple tasks within the terminal rather than use the resources of a mainframe computer.

Intelligent terminals offer various features. One is called *block mode*. In block mode, the mainframe sends information to the terminal specifying fields to be completed. The terminal handles acceptance of the entry of data into the fields, and sometimes also carries out a certain amount of validation. Nothing is sent to the host computer until the user presses the Enter key. At this point all the fields are sent together in a block.

Forms caching is another feature of some intelligent terminals whereby the host computer can request the terminal to save one or more screens in the terminal's memory so that the saved screens can be redisplayed without having to be retransmitted to the terminal. Some terminals also offer a multiple-session capability whereby the user can be logged on to different programs at the same time, and either switch between programs or view them simultaneously in *windows,* or different regions of the screen.

The use of an intelligent terminal can speed up operator input by reducing waiting time, making better use of host computer resources, and making communications more efficient by reducing the number of individual transmissions.

Intelligent terminals as described above are not commonly used in UNIX systems. This is because UNIX software is generally designed to operate with a variety of common terminals, and intelligent features cannot be assumed.

X WINDOWS

X Windows is a system designed at MIT to provide a modern graphical interface for UNIX programs, and to enable the output of multiple programs to be displayed simultaneously on a single screen. Each program can be seen in its own window, and the user can move windows around on the screen and change their size without affecting the operation of the program that is using the particular window. If the user wants to interact with one of the programs, he or she does so by selecting the appropriate window (generally by "clicking" on it with a mouse) and then either typing at the keyboard or using the mouse to select options, draw lines, or paint pictures.

X Windows was primarily designed for work stations running UNIX, connected together via a *local area network* (LAN). An individual work station can display the output of several programs that are running either on the work station itself or on other computers on the network.

Recently, several manufacturers have introduced so-called *X Terminals*. These are terminals that incorporate the X Windows protocol and can be connected via a LAN to a work station to enable several users to share the work station.

TERMINAL EMULATION

With appropriate hardware and software, you can use a microcomputer to emulate a terminal. For example, you could use Crosstalk XVI running on an IBM PC to emulate a DEC VT100 terminal, and use it to connect to a UNIX system.

ADVANTAGES
OF TERMINAL EMULATION

To understand the advantages of using microcomputers as terminals, you only have to wander around the offices of a company that has a mainframe computer, and see the number of desks that have both a microcomputer and a terminal on them. Because terminal emulation allows you to get rid of the terminal and work only with a microcomputer, it pays for itself in space savings alone.

A further advantage of terminal emulation is that you can download data onto a microcomputer, and analyze or otherwise process it locally. For example, you can retrieve sales figures from a corporate database and turn them into a pie chart using Lotus 1-2-3.

Unfortunately, downloading is not always easy. Data formats are not the same on all computers or with different software. Efforts are being made to solve this problem in two ways. Some software developers are producing both mainframe and microcomputer versions of the same product with special facilities for interchange of information. Also, attempts are being made to produce standardized data formats such as IBM's Document Content Architecture (DCA).

TERMINAL EMULATION PROBLEMS

The lack of data security is a major problem related to the downloading of corporate data. This is a constant problem for data-processing departments, and is often very little appreciated by the users. Passwords and access restrictions can be incorporated into the log-on procedures to protect access to sensitive data, but if the information can be saved onto disk it can potentially be stolen by, or inadvertently passed on to, unauthorized persons. This is one reason why data-processing departments often resist the use of microcomputers as terminal emulators.

Other specific areas affecting the feasibility of terminal emulation on a microcomputer are described below.

- The keyboards will almost certainly be different. There may be a disparity in the number of function keys. On a microcomputer there is probably only one key for both Enter and Return. Other keys may be missing and may have to be simulated with awkward combinations of keys pressed together or in sequence.

- The microcomputer may be slower, since it lacks certain dedicated circuitry (for example, scrolling) designed to optimize the performance of a terminal.

- With color terminals the number and combinations of colors may be different from those available with a microcomputer.

- With graphics terminals, the number and scaling of the individual dots may be different in terminal emulation, and the dedicated graphics circuitry may be absent. (Some effects can only be achieved with special chips and architecture.)

- The number of rows and columns may be different, entailing some sort of scrolling or other mechanism that makes the appearance of the microcomputer screen different from that of the original.

- There may be undocumented features of the original terminal that cause unexpected differences in performance; only trial and error can establish the exact way in which the real terminal behaves.

CONNECTING TO
A HOST COMPUTER VIA A LAN

It is becoming more and more common for personal computers to be connected together in *LANs*, or local area networks. Where a LAN is installed, the LAN itself can form part of the connection between an individual personal computer and a host computer. One computer on the network is connected to the host and used as a *communications server*, running software such as NACS (Netware Asynchronous Communications Server). Other computers on the network can then connect to the host by using specially written terminal emulation software that knows how to transmit and receive via the communications server rather than via the regular serial ports. One of my own products, Minisoft 92, enables PCs to communicate with a Hewlett-Packard minicomputer over a LAN in this way, emulating an HP2392A terminal.

The use of communications servers can reduce the number of direct connections that need to be made to the host, and can also enable multiple hosts to be connected to a single LAN, so that individuals can access a variety of hosts without having to change any physical connections.

Figure 6.1 shows a LAN connected to a host via a communications server.

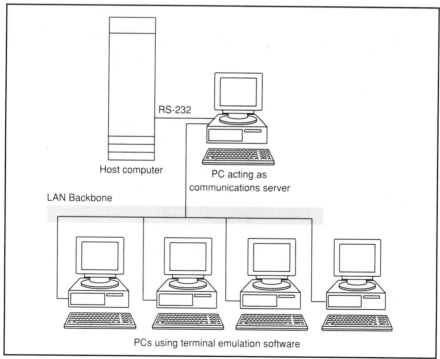

Figure 6.1: Move commands

7

File Transfer

In the course of working with computers, you will find it necessary to transfer files from one computer to another very frequently. Sometimes the receiving computer is intended to process the data in some way. For example, you may have written a letter on a portable computer and want to print it out with another computer that cannot read the same disks. At other times, the second computer is needed merely as a storage device for data that will ultimately be transferred to a third computer. The use of a mainframe as a storage and exchange device is becoming more and more common. When you want to transfer a program or data to another user or to many users, you can upload the data to a central mainframe from which the other users can download it. This happens, for example, with Compu-Serve, when members of a SIG (special interest group) share their programs with other members. It also happens in universities as a means of distributing or transferring software.

Transferring files between computers can serve many purposes, but can also pose many problems. This chapter focuses on the difficulties that can arise during file transfer. Several methods of solving file transfer problems have been devised.

WHY PROTOCOLS ARE NEEDED

Setting up a computer to *transmit* data serially is rather straightforward; almost all computers offer the option of driving a serial printer, and can be programmed to send data out through a serial port without too much difficulty. Most larger computers *receive* serial data all the time because they are controlled through terminals that operate serially.

You would think that in order to transmit data from one computer to another, one must simply make the transmitting computer think that it is printing and make the receiving computer think that it is connected to a terminal. However, it is not quite as simple as that.

The creators of the established methods of computer communication assumed that material would be transferred from a keyboard, in the form of text, and input at human typing speed. File transfers, on the other hand, often take place much faster than a person can type, and sometimes include characters that do not appear on the keyboard. The resulting problems are discussed below.

WORD LENGTH

You will recall that the official ASCII table, which covers the most common keyboard characters, uses only seven-bit words. Much of the data contained in computer files, however, consists of computer programs, graphics data, or other non-ASCII (nontext) material. These data, often referred to as *binary data,* normally use the full eight bits of each byte. Many computer systems and communications channels, designed for ASCII input only, are unable to accept eight-bit words. They insist on seven-bit words, the eighth bit being used as a parity bit. Accordingly, binary data must be converted in some way to seven-bit words before many computer systems will accept them.

CONTROL CHARACTERS

Another problem you may encounter during file transfer involves control characters. Transferred data often contain special byte values that the target computer might misinterpret as ASCII or EBCDIC control signals. Some computers, in fact, will handle special characters in particular ways that cannot be overridden through applications software. In order to overcome this problem, the data must be converted into characters that can be accepted by the receiving computer. Kermit, which was originally devised to facilitate transfers between microcomputers and larger computers, is an example of a protocol that can do this.

BLOCK LENGTH

With many computer systems, input is placed into a buffer before being processed. The size of this buffer is often limited, typically to 128 or 256 bytes. When this is the case, it is not possible to send a lengthy file as a continuous burst of bytes. The sending computer must divide the file and send it as a series of blocks, each of which is smaller than the input buffer of the target machine.

Dividing data into blocks also enables more sophisticated error checking to be carried out, as you will see later in this chapter.

HANDSHAKING

Another item to be aware of is whether different software handshaking procedures may exist on the two machines. For example, XON/XOFF might exist on one but not the other. The use of a file transfer protocol will help to overcome this problem.

ERROR CHECKING

We all experience noisy telephone lines from time to time. However, what appears as noise to us may appear as data to a computer. The longer the transmission and the higher the baud rate, the greater the likelihood of data being corrupted. Therefore it is always advantageous when transferring files to incorporate some form of error checking into your communication.

When the data consist of text, it is generally easy to see where errors have occurred, because the text will look garbled. Where binary data are concerned, however, you can't usually tell what happened. You may know only that your program does not run.

As we have seen in Chapter 2, parity checking is often included in serial communications. However, this check has only a fifty-fifty chance of detecting an error in a single byte, and a single error can be fatal to a computer program in machine-readable form.

Furthermore, after transferring a long file, it is annoying to be told that there has been an error, and have to transfer the whole file again when only part of it is corrupt. It is much better to divide the file into blocks, and have each block checked for errors. That way, your computer will only have to retransmit the corrupted blocks, and your telephone bills will be much lower.

Accordingly, most file transfer protocols divide the data into blocks, and check each block for errors.

FILE TRANSFER PROTOCOLS

There are many different established methods for dealing with the above problems. Some of them are discussed below. Two of them, XMODEM and Kermit, are covered more fully in Appendices B and C. If you are using a commercial communications package, you may well find that a choice of protocols is included. As we will see in Chapter 10, the UUCP system for transferring files between UNIX systems incorporates its own protocols.

HEXADECIMAL CONVERSIONS

A simple way to turn binary data into ASCII transmittable characters is to turn every byte into its hexadecimal equivalent and to transmit the ASCII characters corresponding to each number: two characters for each byte. The whole message will consist of the characters 0 through 9 and A through F. The message is reconverted by the ultimate destination computer (not necessarily the one being used to store the data).

This method solves the problem of sending eight data bits through a seven-bit channel, as well as the problems arising when control characters form part of the data. However, it does not solve the buffering, handshaking, and error-checking problems mentioned above, and it doubles the physical length of the file and therefore the transmission time.

XMODEM

XMODEM is described more fully in Appendix B. It was originally designed for transfers between microcomputers, but it has been used in micro-to-mainframe transfers as well. XMODEM offers error checking, and the division of data into blocks. However, it does not offer the capability of sending eight-bit data through a seven-bit channel, or the conversion of control characters into printable characters.

KERMIT

Kermit is described more fully in Appendix C. It is used primarily for transfers between mainframes and microcomputers and is widely accepted, especially in the academic world. It solves all of the problems described in this chapter.

COMPUSERVE A AND B

These protocols, devised by CompuServe, are used in uploading and downloading data to and from CompuServe. They are offered in some commercial communications packages, as well as in CompuServe's own package.

OTHER FILE TRANSFER CONSIDERATIONS

Following are a few additional items to keep in mind when you are transferring files.

PACKETS AND LAYERS

Both XMODEM and Kermit divide files to be transferred into blocks or packets. Each packet consists of a header of some sort, the data themselves, an error-check code, and an end-of-packet mark. The target computer is expected to send a response indicating whether the packet was correctly received. In the case of XMODEM, this response consists of a single ASCII character returned to the sending device. In the case of Kermit, the response itself is in the form of a packet.

In Chapter 5, we mentioned the general use of packets in telecommunications. There is a big difference, however, between file transfer packets and telecommunications packets.

When telecommunications systems use packets, the packets are generally transparent to each computer. The computers think that they are directly connected, one being a terminal to the other. When running a file transfer protocol such as XMODEM or Kermit, the target computer is aware of the packets, and a program running on the target computer analyzes each packet, checks the error code, strips out the data, and saves them to a file. As a result, the packets being sent under a Kermit file transfer can themselves become the data part of packets being sent through a communications network. These packets can, in turn, become the data part of even higher-level packets. The concept of structures within structures within structures is known as *layering*.

DATA FORMAT

The fact that it may be possible to transfer binary data from one computer to another does not necessarily mean that the second computer will be able to read the data. For example, the data may consist of programs that will not run on the target computer. Even if the two computers use the same processor chip, they may still be designed differently. Even if the two computers are from the same family, the operating systems and memory requirements could still be different. Also, the data may have been created by a program that is not available on the target machine, or by one that is available but works differently on the two machines.

These complications don't matter when you are using the target machine as a storage medium. However, if you want the target machine to process the data in some way, you may have to convert the data.

Some programs, in particular some word-processing, spreadsheet, and database programs, have the ability to read and convert data created by another program. For example, the dBASE series and Lotus 1-2-3 are so prevalent that many software producers make their data formats compatible with those programs.

Attempts are also being made to establish standards for data storage formats, but there are still many cases where the data cannot be used even if they can be transferred.

HALF AND FULL DUPLEX

Half duplex means that both computers do not attempt to communicate at the same time. In other words, at any one time, one computer is in transmitting mode and one is in receiving mode. *Full duplex* means that the computers can both be transmitting at the same time.

When selecting a file transfer method, one of the criteria should be whether or not both computers support full duplex. If they do support full duplex, the receiving computer can send a message concerning successful receipt of a block while receiving a later block. If only half duplex is available, the sending computer has to wait for an acknowledgment after sending each block. This procedure can easily double the transmission time, because waiting for a response to a block often takes longer than transmitting the block.

Another difference between full and half duplex is that with half duplex the characters are not echoed back when they are received. This usually doesn't matter with binary data, but it can be useful to have some real-time evidence that the transmission is being received.

DISK AND TAPE FORMAT CONVERSION

It is sometimes necessary to transfer data between two machines that use the same size disks or the same type of tapes but format them in a different way. Sometimes this is treated as a serial communications problem when, in fact, it can be solved with a simple format conversion program. Programs such as Xeno-copy can read a wide variety of disk formats and convert them to other formats. Clearly this is not possible if the disks are of different sizes or types and the target machine cannot physically read them. But when both machines use 5¼" floppy disks or a standard type of tape, it is often possible to use one of these conversion programs.

Some companies offer a format conversion service to be used when a business is converting from dedicated word-processing machines to personal computers and has a large amount of data to transfer.

I mention the above alternatives just so you will be aware that there are alternative solutions to file transfer problems, and that transferring your data serially is not always the best method.

UNIX Communications for Users

In Part I of this book I presented a general introduction to serial communications. The remainder of the book will deal more specifically with communications under UNIX. Part II will deal with communications for the UNIX user, Part III for the UNIX system administrator, and Part IV for the UNIX programmer.

In Part II, I will start by introducing some general concepts relating to UNIX communications (Chapter 8). In the next three chapters, I will describe three UNIX system utilities that enable you to communicate with other users and other UNIX systems: *mail*, *UUCP*, and *cu*.

8

Introduction
to UNIX
Communications

In this chapter, I will introduce some general concepts relating to UNIX communications.

TARGETS

When discussing UNIX communications, the recipient of a message is often referred to as a *target*. Possible targets include:

- another user on your own host computer
- a user on another machine that is directly connected to your host computer via a serial link or a network
- a user on another machine that can be connected with your host computer via modems
- a user on a machine that can be connected with an intermediate machine that can be connected with your host computer

TARGET IS ON THE SAME MACHINE

The simplest form of communication is where both users are on the same machine. You can use UNIX's *cp* (copy) facility to transfer any type of file, provided that you have access to the directory in which the recipient wants the file to be placed, or you can use *mail* to send a text message. Communication between users on the same machine is illustrated in Figure 8.1.

TARGET IS ON ANOTHER MACHINE

Where the recipient of a message is on another machine, you can use either *mail* or *UUCP* to send the message. In fact, *mail* itself uses *UUCP* to

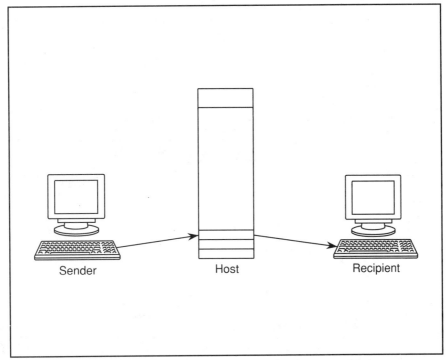

Figure 8.1: Communication between users on the same machine

complete the transfer. You would normally only use the *UUCP* facilities yourself when you want to transfer a non-text file, or to place a file in a specific directory on a target machine. Figure 8.2 illustrates sending a message to a user on another machine.

FORWARDING
MESSAGES TO REMOTE MACHINES

You can also send messages in situations where your machine has no way to contact the recipient's machine directly, but is able to connect to an intermediate machine that can connect to the recipient's machine. This is shown in Figure 8.3.

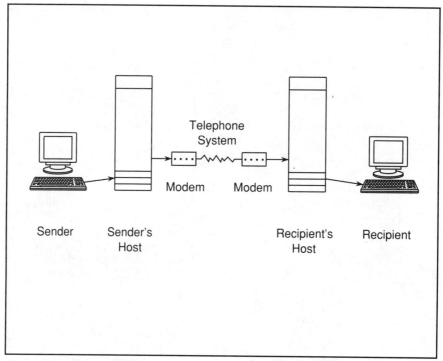

Figure 8.2: Sending a message to a user on another machine

Even more remote transfers can take place, involving several inter-mediate machines. Several thousand UNIX machines are interconnected in this way, and if you know the names of sufficient intermediate machines you can send messages to very many UNIX users around the world. You could even send a message via Australia to the person at the desk next to you. However, this brings us to a very important point. Each time a mes-sage is forwarded, somebody else is paying for the telephone call and, in effect, subsidizing your communications. Without the good will of many other UNIX users, message forwarding would not work. You therefore owe it to the UNIX community not to send unnecessary or lengthy mes-sages or to route them by a longer path than is necessary.

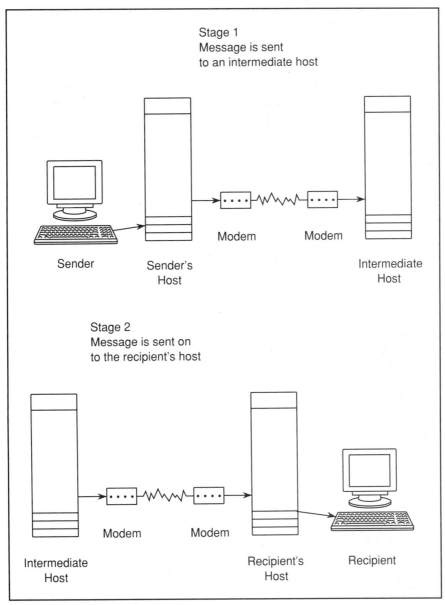

Figure 8.3: Sending a message via an intermediate machine

UNIX ADDRESSES

When you want to send a message to a user on another machine, you need to know the user's address, just as when you send a regular letter. There are two types of address commonly used in the UNIX community: *UUCP*-style addresses, and *Internet-* or *domain*-style addresses. You can recognize *UUCP*-style addresses from the exclamation marks (for example nts!srt!sli!peterg) and Internet-style addresses from the at sign (for example peterg@sli.com). You may have seen business cards with both types of address.

UUCP-STYLE ADDRESSES

When you use *mail* or *UUCP*, you must start by giving the name of a machine that is "known" to your system. (When you configure *UUCP*, you would include the telephone number if the connection is to be made by modem, or the name of the device connecting the two machines if they are directly connected.)

For example, in order to send a message to a user whose log-in name was *jimt* on a machine you know you can communicate with—*sli*—you would address the message *sli!jimt*. However, suppose you want to send a message to a user called *paulag* on a machine that your own machine does not "know"—let's say, *brown*. If you know that the *sli* machine can send messages to *brown* and is willing to do so, you could address the message *sli!brown!paulag*. This process can go further—your message could pass through several machines in a chain before it finally reaches the intended recipient.

When people publish their electronic mail addresses in *UUCP* format, the addresses usually start with the name of one of several very famous machines that are "known" to most UNIX sites. These message hubs perform a valuable public service, and enable you to send messages to a large number of people through the *UUCP* network.

Disadvantages of UUCP-Style Addressing

There are some serious disadvantages to *UUCP*-style addressing:

- **expense** Your addressee might be in the same town or even the same building, and the published address might be through a hub several thousand miles away. It would be expensive to send the message across the country and then back again.

- **delay** With every additional link in the chain between you and the target there will be additional delays. Some machines connect with each other only once a day or even less often. Your recipient may not get the message for several days.

- **risk** There is the possibility that the chain has been broken in some way—one of the machines may be temporarily or permanently unavailable.

INTERNET-STYLE ADDRESSING

The second form of addressing is commonly known as domain- or Internet-style addressing, or Internet format. Internet is a widespread network of U.S. Government and affiliated computers, and the form is used on many networks around the world.

Domain-style addresses are made up as follows:

- the user's name
- the @ symbol
- the host name (usually an abbreviation for the institution or department)
- a period
- the domain name (an indication of the type of institution)

An example would be *peterg@sli.COM*. Here, *peterg* would be the user's name, *sli* would be the institution, and *COM* would indicate that *sli* was a commercial entity. Other domain names are *EDU*, for educational institutions, *GOV* for government institutions, and *MIL* for military organizations. Domain names are often printed in upper case, but the system is not case-sensitive.

The great advantage of this style of addressing is that all host names are officially registered with a central repository (in return for a fee), and that if your machine does not know how to connect with a particular host, it can find out electronically by calling a special number.

Unfortunately, not all UNIX sites can use Internet-style addressing. Special software must be acquired and installed in order to do this, and your own site may not support this facility. In the remainder of this book I will restrict the examples to standard *UUCP*-style addresses.

FURTHER INFORMATION

An excellent book that goes into far greater detail about communicating with non-UUCP networks around the world is *!%@:: A Directory of Electronic Mail Addressing and Networks* by Donnalyn Frey and Rick Adams (Sebastopol, Calif.: O'Reilly and Associates, Inc., 1990).

USENET

USENET is a very widely-used but informal network of UNIX users who exchange news and views via *UUCP*. There are said to be over 150,000 users worldwide. There are over fifty special-interest groups at last count, and at any one time there are ongoing discussions on a large variety of subjects. In order to have access to USENET, you must find a local UNIX site that already has access, and is willing to give you what is known as a *feed*. At regular times your computer will connect to that computer and download new material relating to the *newsgroups* that your site subscribes to. You will also need the *netnews* software. For further information on USENET, I recommend *Using UUCP and USENET* by Grace Todino (1987) and *Managing UUCP and USENET* by Grace Todino and Tim O'Reilly (1990), both published by O'Reilly & Associates, Inc., Sebastopol, California.

UUNET

UUNET is a nonprofit organization that can provide, for a fee, links to USENET, Internet, and other networks. You can contact UUNET at (703) 876-5050.

9

Using UNIX *mail*

Every version of UNIX has a mail facility, designed to enable users of a UNIX system to send messages to each other as well as to other users on remote UNIX systems. Unfortunately, not all the mail programs are the same, and it would not be practicable to cover all the variations here. I'll describe the SCO XENIX *mail*, which is equivalent to the Berkeley *xmail*; if you have a different version of UNIX, you may have to refer to the manual for information specific to your system.

In this chapter, I'll describe

- how *mail* works

- how to send messages

- how to receive and deal with messages

- how to configure *mail*

- how to create *aliases*, which are a useful way of abbreviating names and addresses

HOW MAIL WORKS

Although *mail* has a large number of commands, the fundamental concept is quite simple. Each user has a public mailbox file, stored in the directory /usr/spool/mail. When you want to send a message to a user, you give the name of the user, (for instance, *sally*) and the text of the message to *mail*, which then places the message in Sally's mailbox. She reads her mail from time to time, again using facilities provided by the *mail* program. She can save the message in her private mailbox file in her home directory, or reply to the message, forward it to someone else, or just delete it.

The mechanism for delivering messages depends on the locations of the sender and the recipient.

MESSAGES BETWEEN
USERS ON ONE MACHINE

The simplest case is where both parties are users on the same UNIX host machine. In this case, *mail* can handle the whole transaction by itself, merely adding the new message to the recipient's public mailbox file.

MESSAGES BETWEEN
USERS ON SEPARATE MACHINES

However, *mail* is not restricted to passing messages between users on a single machine. In certain circumstances, it can use the services of *UUCP* to arrange for messages to be sent to users on another machine that is directly connected to the sender's machine or accessible by modem.

FORWARDING
MESSAGES TO REMOTE MACHINES

mail can also use *UUCP* to send messages in situations where the sender's machine has no way to contact the recipient's machine directly, but is able to connect to an intermediate machine that can connect to the recipient's machine.

UUCP AND mail

Where messages must be passed between machines, *mail* calls on the services of another UNIX package, *UUCP*. As mentioned in the last chapter, when you configure *UUCP* you set up details concerning certain other UNIX machines that are "known" to your system. These details would include the telephone number if the connection is to be made by modem, or the name of the device connecting the two machines if they are directly connected. It is important to realize that when *UUCP* is involved, messages are not sent immediately. The messages are *spooled*, or stored in a holding location, until *UUCP* is ready to send them. In some cases *UUCP* will be set up to call a particular machine at a certain time each evening;

in other cases the sending machine may be set up to wait for the addressee's machine to call in before it passes on any relevant messages.

When the *UUCP* connection is made, the messages are passed to the version of *mail* running on the receiving machine. Any message that is directed to a user on the receiving machine is placed in that user's mailbox. Some messages may be addressed to users on other machines, in which case they will be spooled again for onward transmission via *UUCP*.

USING mail

At its simplest, *mail* can be used interactively. Just type mail followed by the user-ID of the person you want to send the message to, for example

    mail jim

mail will place you into *compose mode*, which allows you type in the *header* of the message and the message itself. You complete the message by pressing Ctrl-D, and the message is sent. Next time Jim logs on, or uses the mail command himself, he will be told that he has mail, and will be able to read your message. He reads his mail by typing mail without any parameters. mail shows him a list of headers for any mail he has not yet disposed of, and places him in command mode. He can now reply to your message or otherwise dispose of it.

SENDING MESSAGES WITH mail

A *mail* message consists of a header followed by the body of the message. I will deal with each of these in turn.

THE HEADER

The header consists of

- a list of one or more addressees (preceded by *To:*)
- a list of persons to receive copies (preceded by *Cc*)

- the user-ID of the person to receive notification of delivery
- the subject (preceded by *Subject:*)

The Addressee(s)

As we saw above, you can enter the name of the addressee of your message at the time you invoke *mail* simply by adding the name after the mail command. If you want the message to go to more than one addressee, simply add their names to the list. For example:

    mail jim bill sally

By using the ~t command, you can also add the names of the recipients after you have started *mail*. As we will see, *mail* has a number of commands starting with a *tilde* (the ~ character). Tilde commands must be given at the beginning of a new line. For example, to add Maria to the list of recipients, enter

    ~t maria

on a new line.

If the message you are sending is to be read from a disk file, the tilde commands can be contained in the file. We will see later in this chapter how to instruct *mail* to read a disk file.

Although you can use ~t to add recipients, you cannot use it to remove them. However, you can alter anything in the header section of the message by using the ~h command, as we will see later.

As well as sending messages to other people on the same system, you can send messages to people on remote systems. Later in this book, we will deal extensively with how UNIX systems can pass messages between themselves. For now all you need to understand is that your UNIX system can be configured in such a way that it knows how to send messages to "known" remote sites. For example, if your system knows how to send messages to a site called *sli* via *UUCP*, and you want to send a message to a person who is a user of the sli machine with the user-ID *jim*, you can make the addressee of the message

    sli!jim

mail will send the message to Jim at the *sli* site.

If your system does not know how to send messages to the *sli* site, but knows how to communicate with a site called *nt*, and you know that *nt* knows how to communicate with *sli*, you can address the message

    nt!sli!jim

If you wish to see a list of sites that your system can communicate with via *UUCP*, enter

    uuname

(This will not list the sites that you can send messages to *indirectly*, because this could conceivably number in the thousands.)

Copies and Blind Copies

You can send a message that is primarily addressed to Jim, but with *copies* to Bob and Sally. You would start as if the message were going only to Jim, as follows:

    mail jim

Once you are in compose mode, you can request copies to Bob and Sally by using the ~c command:

    ~c bob sally

If you do not want Jim to know that you are sending copies to Bob and Sally, you would user the ~b command for *blind copy*, in place of the ~c command.

Receipt of Delivery

You can ask for notification that a message has been delivered to a user by using the ~Return command—for example,

    ~Return peterg

The Subject

The *subject* of a message is a short description that will appear in the heading when the addressee reads a list of his incoming mail. It is always helpful to add a subject field, as it helps recipients in determining priorities when they review their mail.

There are two ways to add a subject. First, *mail* is often set up to prompt you for the subject. For example, when you enter

    mail jim

mail responds with "Subject:?" See the section on customizing *mail* below for how to set up *mail* to prompt for the subject every time you address a message.

Second, you can enter a new subject by using the ~s command as in the following example:

    ~s Sales Meeting

You can also use the ~s command within a message that you create using an editor. Finally, by using the -s option, you can add the subject to the command line when you invoke *mail:*

    mail jim -s Sales Meeting

Another Way to Change the Header

The header in *mail* consists of the list of addressees (starting with *To:*), followed by the subject (starting with *Subject:*), the list of persons to receive copies (starting with *Cc:*), and the user-ID of the person to receive return receipt (starting with *Return-receipt-to*).

You can edit the header one line at a time by typing

    ~h

This will cause *mail* to display "To:" followed by the list of recipients. The cursor will be placed at the end of the line. You can use the normal editing keys to change this line. *mail* will then display "Subject:" followed by the subject, and the other lines making up the header. You can edit each of these lines as you wish.

THE BODY OF THE MESSAGE

Having explained how to specify the header of the message, I will now describe how to enter the message itself. The following methods are available:

- interactively, when prompted by *mail*
- including a pre-written text file
- invoking an editor program from within *mail*

Note that whichever approach you take, you can include in the body of the message the various tilde commands to change the heading.

Entering the Body of the Message Interactively

The quickest way to send a message is simply to type the body of the message in response to *mail's* prompt. However, the editing facilities are limited, and it can be easier to write the message in advance or to branch to a text editor from within *mail*.

Sending a Pre-Written Message

You can write a message in advance using a text editor such as *vi*. Suppose that you have created a letter and saved it with the file name *meeting*. You can then mail the message by using the redirect sign as follows:

```
mail jim < meeting
```

You can also ask *mail* to read in a text file in compose mode, by using the ~r command. For example, to read in a text file called *letter*, enter

```
~rletter
```

Invoking an Editor from within mail

You can use an external text editor from within *mail*. Simply go to a new line and type ~e (for edit) or ~v (for *vi*, but also used for any other editor you have defined using the VISUAL option, as described later under "Customizing *mail*"). You will be able to create your message using your favorite editing program. When you exit from the editor, you will automatically return to *mail* and can continue to add lines, or to send the message.

Finally, you can include a message that you started to edit but abandoned. When you abort the creation of a message, *mail* saves the current message in a file called *dead.letter* in your home directory. To include that file in a new message, simply type ~r without a file name.

READING YOUR mail

Having described how to send mail to other people, I will now describe how to read your mail once it has been received.

NOTIFICATION THAT YOU HAVE mail

When somebody sends a message to you using *mail*, it is held in a special directory until you choose to read and dispose of it.

There are four ways in which you can find out that you have mail:

- when you log on
- when new mail arrives and you are at a system prompt (some systems)
- by using the mail command without an addressee
- when you are actually running *mail* at the time a new message arrives

When you log on to UNIX, if there is mail in your in-box you will receive a message such as "You have mail." This does not necessarily mean that the mail is new. It may be that you have read it, but not deleted it.

With some UNIX systems, you can arrange to be notified when new mail is received. With XENIX, you do this by setting the *MAIL* system variable if you are using the Bourne shell, or the *mail* system variable if you are using the C shell.

When you enter the mail command on its own, *mail* will tell you how many messages are waiting for you.

READING YOUR MAIL

In order to read your mail, you will normally use the mail command without any parameters. *mail* will start by telling you how many messages are pending, and will display the headers of the most recent messages, starting with the newest. Each message header is given a number, with the highest number first.

You do not have to read your messages in sequence. The normal procedure is to scan through the message headers and decide, depending on the sender and the message subject, which messages you want to deal with first. If you have a lot of mail, there may be more headers than can appear on the screen at one time. You can scan through the message headers by using the commands in Table 9.1.

Table 9.1: Commands for Viewing Headers

COMMAND	PURPOSE
h	Show the current group of headers
h+	Show the next group of headers, if there are too many to show on the screen at one time
h-	Show the previous group of headers
restart	Show headers including those for any new mail that has arrived during your *mail* session

Displaying Messages

When you find a message that you want to read, you can ask *mail* to display it on the screen. The commands in Table 9.2 are available for displaying messages that appear in your message list.

The *current message* is the message for the most recently displayed header.

Table 9.2: Commands for Displaying Messages

COMMAND	PURPOSE
Return key	Display the current message
p	Display the current message
p*	Display all messages
+	Display the next message
n	Display the next message
n	Display message number *n*
^	Display the first message
$	Display the last message
+*n*	Go forward *n* messages
—	Display the previous message
—*n*	Go back *n* messages

Acting On the Message

Once you have read a message, you can take several actions with respect to it. You can reply to it, forward it to a third person, copy it to a file, delete it, or leave it in the mailbox to be dealt with later. The commands in Table 9.3 allow you to deal with messages. In this table, *m* indicates the list of one or more messages to be acted on.
A message list can be

- **a single message number** For example, to delete message 1 type

  d 1

- **a list of message numbers** To delete messages 1, 3, and 5 type

  d 1 3 5

- **a range of message numbers** To reply to messages 4 through 6, type

  r 4-6

- **all messages from a particular person** To save all the messages from Jim in a file called jim_mail, type

  s jim jim_mail

Table 9.3: Commands for Acting on a Message

COMMAND	ACTION
dp	Deletes the current message and displays the next one
d *m*	Deletes the messages specified by *m*
u *m*	Undeletes the messages specified by *m*
v *m*	Edits the messages specified by *m* with the *vi* editor
e *m*	Edits the messages specified by *m* with the *ed* text editor
f *user(s)*	Forwards the current message to the named users, indenting it within a new message
F *user(s)*	Forwards the current message to the named users, without indentation
s *m fname*	Saves the messages specified by *m* into a mailbox-format file with the specified name. This option is available under SCO UNIX but not under SCO XENIX
w *fname*	Writes the body of the current message to a text-format file with the specified name
mb *m*	Saves the messages specified by *m* in the user's private mailbox
r	Reply. You can then enter the text of the reply just as if you had entered *mail* giving as the addressee the author of the message you are replying to
R	Reply as above, but sending copies of the reply to the people who received copies of the original. People who received blind copies of the original will not receive copies of the reply

OTHER mail COMMANDS

Several other commands are available to you while you are using *mail* in command mode. You can use these commands while you are reading and dealing with your messages. These commands are shown in Table 9.4.

Table 9.4: Additional *mail* Commands

COMMAND	ALTERNATIVE	MEANING
?	list	Help: lists the commands
alias		See the section on aliases below
cd		Change the current directory, the same as the UNIX **cd** command
x	exit	Exit from *mail* without saving any changes
q	quit	Exit from *mail* saving changes
se	set	Set an option (See section on customizing *mail* below)
uns	unset	Cancel an option (See section on customizing *mail* below)
string *str m*		Search for the string *str* in the message list *m*
whois		Look up and display the real name of a message recipient

CUSTOMIZING mail

You can adapt *mail* to your own preferences by setting a number of variables. These variables can be set interactively during a *mail* session, using the set and unset commands.

For convenience, you can store a list of your preferred variables and settings in a file. When *mail* starts up, it reads two files. The first is /usr/lib/mail/mailrc. This file will normally be maintained by the system administrator, and will contain options common to all users. The second file is the file .mailrc in each user's home directory. For example, my own file is /usr/peterg/.mailrc. This file contains options specific to that user. Since the individual file is read after the common file, commands in the individual file can override commands in the common file.

VARIABLES THAT CONTAIN TEXT

EDITOR *fname*	The name of the text editor to use when the e, edit, or ~e command is used
SHELL *pathname*	The path name of the shell to use when a new shell is requested
VISUAL *fname*	The name of the text editor to use when the v, visual or ~v command is used
alias *short long*	The short version of a name to be used in place of a longer *UUCP* path (for example, nt!scl!sli!peterg) or a group of user names or addresses
escape *character*	When composing mail, the character specified is accepted in place of the tilde (~) character
page=*n*	When displaying messages, *n* lines of text are displayed in a page
record *fname*	Saves all outgoing mail in a mailbox-format file with the path *fname*. This file can be read with the mail command
toplines=*n*	When the command top is used, displays *n* lines of each message

SWITCHES

The following variables that do not contain text are called *switches:*

askcc	At the end of each message that you enter, *mail* will prompt you for additional people to receive carbon copies
asksubject	*mail* will prompt you for the subject each time you send a message
autombox	Messages that you do not read will be saved in your personal mailbox instead of in the system mailbox
autoprint	Each time you delete a message using the command d (delete) the next message will be displayed. This makes the d command work in the same way as the dp command
chron	Messages are displayed starting with the oldest instead of the newest
dot	Allows you to use a period at the end of a message to indicate the end of the file
execmail	Messages you send will be transmitted as a background process so that you can continue entering new messages at the same time
ignore	Interrupt signals from your terminal will be ignored and echoed as at signs (@)
mchron	Messages will be listed starting with the most recent, but displayed starting with the oldest
metoo	When mail is sent to a group, and the sender is a member of the group, the sender will receive the mail. (Without this switch, the sender would be removed from the list)

nosave	Aborted messages are not saved in the dead letter file in the user's home directory
quiet	*mail* will not display its version header when it starts up
verify	*mail* will check to see that each addressee is a valid user

ALIASES

A very useful feature of *mail* is the ability to create *aliases,* which are abbreviations that you can use for people to whom you often send mail.

WHAT ALIASES REPRESENT

An alias can represent an individual or a group. For example, you could declare the alias *jim* to represent nt!slc!sli!jimb. From then on, you could enter simply

    mail jim

and *mail* would expand this to

    mail nt!slc!sli!jimb

You could also define, for example, *partners* to represent *bill jack sally.* Then you could enter

    ~cc partners

and *mail* would expand this to

    ~cc bill jack sally

DECLARING ALIASES

You can declare aliases in the following ways:

In Your Personal .mailrc Startup File   This file is described in the previous section ("Customizing *mail*"). You can enter one or more aliases, and these will be available to you each time you use *mail*. Each alias starts on a new line. For example, your .mailrc might contain the following lines:

    alias jim hp!slc!jimb

    alias friends bill bob sue

    alias mygroup sally billf roger

In the System .mailrc File   Aliases placed here can be used by all users. It is advantageous to use system-wide aliases where possible, since if a contact's UUCP address changes all you need to do is change the alias entry. The users can continue to send mail to that person using the same alias.

In Compose Mode   While you are composing mail, you can set an alias temporarily by using the ~alias command. For example:

    ~alias jim ntx!sli!jimb

This alias will apply until you quit *mail,* and then it will be forgotten.

In Interactive Mode   You can use the alias command while using *mail* in interactive mode exactly the same as using ~alias in compose mode.

LISTING YOUR ALIASES

You sometimes want to see a list of the aliases that are currently set. To do this, use the command alias in interactive mode or ~alias in compose mode, without any arguments. A list of your aliases will be displayed.

You can also find out what the expansion of a particular alias is. For example, you can enter (in interactive mode)

    alias jim

and *mail* will respond

    alias jim ntx!sli!jimb

10

Using *UUCP*

In the last chapter, I described how you can use *mail* to send messages to other users at your site, and in certain circumstances to users at other sites. When you send a message to a remote site, *mail* itself uses the facilities provided by UUCP (short for Unix to Unix Copy). UUCP was designed to facilitate transferring files between UNIX sites, and can be used for purposes other than simply transferring messages.

There are several versions of UUCP. The version described here is known as Honey DanBer UUCP, after the designers Peter Honeyman, David A. Norwitz and Brian E. Redman. In this Chapter I will describe the UUCP commands used most often. In a later chapter I will describe the commands used by system administrators to install and configure UUCP.

INTRODUCTION TO UUCP

UUCP consists of a set of programs for transmitting and receiving files between UNIX systems. You can also use UUCP to execute commands on a remote system. Using UUCP, you can communicate with any of the following:

- a UNIX machine directly connected with your own (for example, two machines serving separate departments in the same building)
- a UNIX machine accessible from your machine using a modem
- a UNIX machine accessible from another machine that is accessible to·yours

Files are generally not transferred immediately: usually your machine will dial up a particular target machine at regular times, perhaps once a day, in order to exchange messages.

In order to use UUCP, you must first install the UUCP package. You must also record information about each site, or target machine, with which you want to communicate. I will describe the installation and setup of UUCP in Chapter 16.

The following is a list of programs forming the part of UUCP that you are likely to use as a regular UNIX user. Notice that the first one is called *uucp*. To distinguish the program *uucp* from the complete package UUCP, the program is always shown in lower case.

uucp	Transmits and receives files
uuto	Another way to transmit files
uupick	Retrieves files sent to you
uux	Executes programs at a remote site
uustat	Indicates the current UUCP status
uuencode	Translates binary files into ASCII
uudecode	Translates ASCII files into binary
uuname	Lists machines with which your machine can connect

TRANSFERRING FILES WITH uucp

The syntax of the uucp command is very much like that of the cp command. The formal definition is as follows:

uucp *[options] sourcemachine!sourcefile targetmachine!targetfile*

You give the name of the source machine, the name of the file you want to transmit, and the machine name, and path indicating where you want the file to be stored on the target machine. You can also set certain optional flags.

BEFORE YOU CAN TRANSMIT

Before you can send a file to a remote machine, or request a file from a remote machine, you must first establish whether that machine is "known" to your machine. You can find this out by entering

uuname

This will display a list of machines, or sites, with which your computer can connect. Second, you must ensure that the target machine is set up to receive UUCP messages from your machine. You will recall that with the mail command, you can send messages to users on machines that you cannot directly connect with, if you know that a machine that you *can* connect with can itself connect with the addressee's machine. You can do the same thing with uucp and uuto, as we will see.

Next, you must ensure that the file you want to send is enabled for read access by third parties, and that the directory containing the file is enabled for both read and execute access.

Finally, you must ensure that the directory on the remote machine to which you are sending the file is enabled for write access by third parties. If you are unsure of this, or do not know of a suitable directory on the remote machine, you can send the file to a general UUCP directory, as described in the next section.

THE SOURCE
MACHINE AND FILE NAME

You specify the source machine and file name as follows:

sourcemachine!filename

When you transmit a file from your own machine to a remote machine, you do not specify the source machine's name, and can omit the full path of the file if the file is in your current directory. When you request a file from a remote machine, you must give the machine name and the full path of the file.

THE TARGET
MACHINE AND FILE NAME

You specify the target machine and file name as follows:

targetmachine!filename

The Target Machine

The variable *targetmachine* must be the name of a machine that is known to your computer. If you are not sure whether a particular machine is known to your computer, you can use the uuname command, which lists all the machines that your computer can connect with directly. Incidentally, you can find out the name of your own computer by typing

    uuname -l

The Target File Name and Directory

The variable *filename* indicates the name under which the file will be stored on the target machine, as well as the directory in which it will be placed. There are four possible forms for *filename:*

- **full pathname** The file will be placed in the directory that you specify. This will only work if the directory in question is enabled for writing by others. For security reasons, many sites do not allow UUCP transfers except into certain directories specially set up for UUCP.

- **no pathname** The file will be placed in the directory on the target machine corresponding to the directory on the source machine. The same restrictions apply as under full pathname above.

- **public directory** If you do not know of a suitable directory on the target machine, you can request that the file be placed in a special general directory on the target machine. You do this by using the tilde sign (~) as follows:

    target!~/file

  When you use this form, the UUCP package at the receiving computer will place the file in the directory /usr/spool/uucppublic.

- **user's login directory** Suppose that your are sending a file to a user named George on a machine called *sli.* George's login name on the target machine is *georgeb*. His login directory is /usr/george. If you designate the target as follows:

```
sli!~george/data/nfile
```

then the file will be stored in a directory /usr/george/data, with the file name *nfile*.

Forwarding Transfers

As I mentioned above, you can request an intermediate machine to forward a transfer to a destination machine. For example, suppose that your machine can communicate with a machine called *sli*, and *sli* can communicate with a machine called *sco*. You can send a message to the *sco* machine as in the following example:

```
uucp myfile sli!sco!/usr/jimb/myfile
```

You can go beyond a single intermediate machine, and have the message pass through several machines in turn. These chains can get quite long at times.

If you are requesting a file from a remote system, rather than sending a file from your own machine, the target machine will be your own and you should omit the machine name. For example,

```
uucp sli!/usr/peterg/sourcefile targetfile
```

You will not be able to request a file from a remote system unless your system has permission to download files; for security reasons this right is often limited. See Chapter 16 for more information.

uucp OPTIONS

Several options can be added to the uucp command. For example, -m asks *uucp* to send you mail and indicate whether the transfer was successful or not, and -nuser asks *uucp* to notify the user on the remote machine when the file has been transferred. There are other options available, but they are primarily of interest to system administrators, and require knowledge of how UUCP works.

SENDING FILES WITH uuto

The program *uuto* is another way in which files can be transferred from one computer to another. It is simpler than *uucp,* but has fewer options.

The formal definition of the uuto command is

uuto *sourcefile targetmachine!login*

sourcefile is the name of the file that you want to transmit. If it is not in your current directory, you must specify a path. *sourcefile* must set read permission for others, and the directory containing *sourcefile* must set read and execute permission for others. *targetmachine* is the name of the machine to which you want to transmit the file. As with *uucp,* the target machine must be "known" to your machine. *login* is the login name of the person to whom you want to send the file.

When the target machine receives the file, it places it in a special directory set up for the user that you specified with the *login* parameter. For example, if your machine is known as *nj* and you transmitted the file with the following command—

uucp myfile sli!peterg

—the receiving machine (*sli*) will place the file in the directory /usr/spool/uucppublic/receive/peterg/nj.

At the same time, mail will be sent to peterg indicating that the file has been received. This is equivalent to the -n option for *uucp.* You can also request that you receive an indication via *mail* of the success or failure of the transfer by using *uuto's* -m option. Note that if you receive a message that the file was successfully transferred, all this means is that the file now exists on the target machine. It does not necessarily mean that the addressee has read the mail and knows that the file is there.

Remember that, like *uucp* and *mail*, *uuto* does not transmit files immediately. They might be sent once a day or even less frequently, when your machine connects with the target machine.

RECEIVING FILES WITH uupick

The program *uupick* enables you to search for files that have been sent to you via *uuto*. You will recall that these files are placed in the subdirectory /usr/spool/uucppublic/receive/*login*/*sourcemachine*. (*login* once again is the user login name of the recipient.) To search for files that have been sent to you, simply enter

    uupick

If any files are found, *uupick* will display the name of each one in turn in the following format:

    from *sourcemachine: file filename ?*

The question mark indicates that *uupick* wants instructions as to what to do with the file that has been found. The following responses are available:

m *[dir]*	Move the file (to the optional specified directory)
d	Delete the file
q	Quit *uupick*

THE uustat COMMAND

As I mentioned at the beginning of this chapter, UUCP does not transmit files immediately. From time to time it will connect with a particular target machine, and transmit at one time all the files that have accumulated for that machine. You may sometimes wonder whether a particular file has yet been transmitted. You can find this out by using the uustat command. Simply type uustat, and you will see a list of your current jobs, in the following format:

2221	jim	sli	5/24-9:30	5/25-9:45	JOB IS QUEUED
2222	bob	sco	5/24-9:45	5/25-9:45	JOB IS QUEUED

As you can see, there are six items shown for every job listed:

1. job number
2. requestor
3. target machine
4. date and time spooled
5. current date and time
6. status

The format on your system may differ, depending on your version of *uucp*, but the basic information will be similar.

TRANSFERRING BINARY FILES

In Chapter 2, I explained the difference between ASCII and binary files. Like *mail*, *uucp* can only be used to transfer ASCII files. However, two UUCP utility programs are available that convert binary files into ASCII and vice versa. These programs are *uuencode* and *uudecode*.

To convert a binary file called *binfile* into an ASCII file called *ascfile*, type

```
uuencode < binfile > ascfile
```

If you receive a file called *ascfile* that has been converted from binary, you can convert it back by typing

```
uudecode < ascfile > binfile
```

Once a file has been translated into ASCII, it can be sent with *mail*, *uucp*, or *uuto*. The file will be about one third longer as an ASCII file than it was as a binary file.

There is a way in which you can ask the receiving UUCP to decode the file automatically upon receipt, by addressing the file using *decode* as the user's name. However, not all UNIX installations support this facility.

THE uux COMMAND

The command uux enables you to request commands to be executed on a target machine. For example, a computer at the head office of a large company could call computers at each branch office and request the local computers to generate reports of the day's trading figures. Alternatively, you could check that a user at another site had the most recent copy of a document by requesting the remote computer to run the diff command to compare it with a copy on your own computer. By using the UNIX redirect symbol (>), you can request the output of the program to be sent to a file on your own computer. As with the other UUCP commands, uux is not executed immediately, but only when your computer connects with the particular target computer.

As you can imagine, a computer that allowed any command to be executed by a remote computer could be very vulnerable to sabotage and other security breaches. For this reason, most sites severely restrict what commands received from another site will be obeyed. I will describe these procedures in Chapter 16, "Configuring UUCP."

The format of the uux command is as follows:

uux *[options] commandline*

For example, you could obtain a directory listing of a directory on a remote system as follows:

uux "!ls sli!/usr/peterg > !listfile"

This command would execute the ls command on the remote computer, and redirect the results to a file called *listfile* on your own machine. The exclamation point is an abbreviation for your own machine.

11

Connecting
with *cu*

I described in the last chapter how you can use UUCP to transfer files between two UNIX systems and, with some limitations, execute commands on a remote UNIX system. Sometimes you may want to do more than this. You may want to log on to a remote system as a user. You will, of course, first need to be set up with a name and password by the system administrator of the remote system. Assuming you have got this far, there are several ways in which you can proceed. Because *cu* (for "call UNIX") is provided with UNIX, I will start by describing that program. I will explain the various *cu* commands, and present a sample session. I will then discuss some alternatives to *cu*.

CONNECTING WITH cu

cu is designed to enable you to connect to a second computer (normally, but not necessarily, running UNIX) from within UNIX without terminating your current session. *cu* will first make the connection, then route what you type to the second computer, and route the output from the second computer to your screen. Certain special keystrokes will be intercepted by *cu* so that you can execute local commands and request file transfers between the two systems.

Figure 11.1 shows the connections made during a typical *cu* session. In the example, the user's terminal is connected to a local host computer running UNIX, and the local host computer is connected via modems to a remote computer. Other configurations are possible: the second computer could be directly connected to the first, as with two computers in the same building, for example. You can even use *cu* to connect to a remote UNIX system, and then run *cu* on the remote system to connect to a third system.

MAKING THE CONNECTION

The command to make a connection with a remote system is cu itself, followed by a number of optional parameters. You can identify a remote

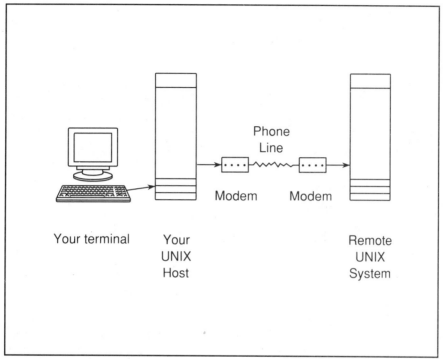

Figure 11.1: Configuration of a typical *cu* session

system by name, in which case *cu* will look at the appropriate UUCP files to find out how to connect to that particular system. Alternatively, you can specify the telephone number, baud rate, and other communications parameters on the command line.

Communications Parameters

In the first part of this book, I explained the various communications parameters such as baud rate and parity. *cu* allows you to specify baud rate and parity on the command line. The applicable options are

-sspeed   Speed (baud rate). *Speed* will be one of the following: 150, 300, 600, 1200, 2400, 4800, 9600, 19200, 38400

-o	Seven data bits with odd parity
-e	Seven data bits with even parity
-oe	Seven data bits, ignoring parity
-h	Half duplex. Anything you type will be echoed locally on your screen. The default is full duplex, where it is assumed that the remote system will echo characters

The baud rate will be ignored if you specified a UUCP system name to call, since the baud rate for each known system was recorded when the system was added to your UUCP configuration. If you omit the parity settings, eight data bits and no parity will be assumed.

The following example sets 1200 baud, even parity and half duplex:

cu -s1200 -e -h *[other options]*

Telephone Number

You can specify a telephone number to call by adding the number to the command line. An equals sign (=) in the number asks *cu* to wait for a second dial tone before proceeding. This would enable you, for example, to dial 9 for an outside line and then dial the actual number, as in the following example:

cu *[other options]* 9=14091112222

You can also include one or more hyphens to require *cu* to wait for four seconds before continuing.

Device Name

I have not yet dealt with UNIX device names and device drivers in this book. These will be covered in Part III. However, for completeness I should mention here that each serial port on a UNIX system is given a special name and that you can require *cu* to use a particular port by specifying its name. This can be useful if you know that a particular system is directly connected to your host via a particular port. The command to use the device /dev/tty1a would be

cu -l /dev/tty1a *[other options]*

System Name

Although *cu* is not part of UUCP, it can read the UUCP files that specify the names of known systems. If you specify a known system name, you do not need to specify communications parameters such as baud rate, parity, or telephone number. To use a system name, simply add the name as a parameter to the cu command. For example, if you have a system set up called *cis* you can instruct *cu* to call cis by typing

cu cis

Unfortunately, *cu* will not follow the log-on instructions specified for that system in the UUCP *Systems* file. You will still have to log on manually.

NOTE

Advanced users can automate logging on through *cu* by creating a custom dialer file that logs on after making the connection. Dialer files are presented in Chapter 16.

Other Command-Line Options

There are three final options to the cu command that are less frequently used. They are as follows:

-xn   Used for debugging purposes. Details of the program execution are printed at the current error listing device. *n* is a number from 1 to 9 indicating the debugging level. It is normally set to 9.

-n   The user will be prompted to enter the telephone number at the keyboard.

dir   The user will be connected with the device
                 specified with the –l option. The enables you, for
                 example, to send special commands to a modem
                 to set it up.

EXECUTING LOCAL COMMANDS

While you are engaged in a session with a remote computer using *cu*,
you may sometimes want to run a command on your local machine
without disconnecting the remote session. For example, you may want to
check to see whether you have received any urgent mail. There are three
ways in which you can do this:

~!cmd   instructs *cu* to run the command cmd

~!   escapes to a new shell on your local machine. You will see a new
UNIX prompt and can execute one or more commands from within
the new shell. When you have finished, you will press Ctrl-D to terminate the shell, and you will be returned to your remote session

~$cmd   instructs *cu* to run the command cmd and redirect its output
to the remote system

SENDING AND RECEIVING FILES

You can instruct *cu* to send or receive an ASCII file to or from the
remote system. *cu* will use UNIX commands on the remote system, so you
cannot use this facility if the remote system is not running UNIX.
The commands to send and receive files are

~%put -   sends the file *sourcefname* and saves it on the
sourcefname   remote system as *targetfname*
[targetfname]

~%take   requests the remote system to send the file
sourcefname   *sourcefname* and save it on your local system as
[targetfname] *targetfname*

In both cases, *targetfname* can be omitted, in which case the file will be saved with the same name as the source file.

You may want to send a text file to a remote computer that is not running UNIX. For example, you may want to upload a message to CompuServe. In order to do this, you would first instruct CompuServe to start capturing text. You would then instruct *cu* to transmit the file by typing the following:

```
~$cat sourcefname
```

In the above example, we instructed *cu* to run the UNIX command cat and redirect its output to the remote system. *cat* is a UNIX program that in this instance will simply copy the file *sourcefname* to standard output.

CAPTURING A COMPLETE SESSION

You may sometimes want to capture a complete communications session in a file. You can do this by using the UNIX tee command, which enables you to take the output of a program (in this case, *cu*) and send it to both its standard output and another destination (in this case, your screen and a file). Let's assume that you have specified the phone number and other parameters for a system known as *cis* using UUCP. You can call *cis* and capture the session in the file *ciscap* by typing the following:

```
cu cis | tee ciscap
```

DISCONNECTING

When you have finished with your communications session, you can terminate the *cu* session by typing

```
~.
```

Remember to log off the remote computer appropriately first. With some systems, terminating the communications link does not automatically terminate the session. If you disconnect without logging off, there are two potential problems. Firstly, you may continue to incur connect charges, and secondly the next user to call in on the same number may be connected to your session without even knowing your password.

Many systems automatically hang up the telephone line when you log off. If this happens, and *cu* detects that the carrier signal has been lost, *cu* will automatically terminate and you will not have to instruct it to quit.

OTHER cu COMMANDS

These are some remaining commands that you can use:

~%break	Transmit a break signal to the remote computer
~~line	Transmit the line *line* to the remote computer
~%cd	Change the current directory on the local system. You should use this command rather than ~!cd, because that way *cu* would invoke a new shell to execute the cd command, the shell would then be closed, and your current directory would be as it was before you executed the command.
~nostop	Change to and from DC1/DC3 (XON/XOFF) input control, so that you can conform to the requirements of the remote system

SAMPLE cu SESSION: COMPUSERVE

CompuServe is a very popular online service that offers "forums" on very many subjects, and access to a large number of databases. One of the forums is the UNIX Forum, whereby you can read messages, participate in online discussions, and download files pertaining to UNIX. In order to access CompuServe, you first need to buy a subscription, and you will be allocated a number and a password; the first thing you do, of course, will be to change your password. You are then charged by the hour for the time you are online.

You can access CompuServe using *cu*. I recommend that you set up an entry in *Systems* (see Chapter 16, "Configuring UUCP") for *cis*, giving your local access number for CompuServe. Then connect with CompuServe, capturing the session by typing

    cu cis | tee ciscp

When you get a message from your modem that you are connected, press Ctrl-C. CompuServe will then prompt you for your user-ID and password. Once you have entered these, you will see the main CompuServe menu. To reach the UNIX Forum, type

    GO UNIXFORUM

You can then read the messages, download files, and so on. However, many of the files are in binary format, and you cannot download these using *cu*. In order to do this you will need a communications program that offers binary file transfer protocols such as XMODEM or Kermit. You could consider PRO-YAM, or XCMALT, a public-domain program that you can download (in ASCII form) from CompuServe.

CompuServe also offers an interface to Internet via its electronic mail system. If you do not have a connection, you can send messages to Internet addresses by addressing them to

    >INTERNET:*nnnn@ccccc.aaa*

where *nnnn* is the name, *ccccc* is the organization, and *aaa* is the extension. Internet users can likewise send messages to CompuServe users by addressing them to

    xxxxx.yyyy@compuserve.com

where *xxxxx.yyyy* is the CompuServe user-ID. Note that CompuServe IDs consist of two numbers separated by a comma, but for Internet purposes you must substitute a period for the comma.

When you have finished with your CompuServe session, you exit from CompuServe by typing

    OFF

CompuServe will drop the line, and *cu* will probably recognize the loss of carrier and quit. If *cu* does not quit, you can force it to by typing

~.

ALTERNATIVES TO cu

I will now discuss some alternatives to using the *cu* program.

DIALING DIRECTLY FROM YOUR TERMINAL

First, you can attach a modem to your terminal and dial up the remote system instead of your regular computer. This is the simplest method. However, there are several disadvantages to this approach:

- You would have to disconnect from your main computer in order to connect with the remote computer

- You could not transfer files between the remote computer and your local computer

- The remote system might not have dial-in facilities: it may be accessible only through a direct link to your main computer (such as via Internet)

- You might not have access to a modem or a suitable telephone line

DIALING DIRECTLY FROM YOUR PERSONAL COMPUTER

If you normally use a personal computer rather than a terminal to connect to your regular UNIX host, you will be using a terminal emulation program such as Crosstalk XVI (for IBM PCs and compatibles) or Microphone II (for Macintosh computers). You may be able to use the same program and equipment to access the remote system. Most of the disadvantages listed above for terminals still apply. You will, however, be able to transmit and receive files, although if the files originate from or are destined for your UNIX system a second file transfer will have to take place between your PC and your regular host.

USING KERMIT

I mentioned the Kermit file transfer protocol in Chapter 7. Kermit also exists as a communications program that you can use to connect with remote systems, and versions are available for many different computers. It is primarily designed for file transfer, rather than interactive sessions, but if file transfer is what you need Kermit will probably do the job. Most implementations have facilities for automated log-on and transferring multiple files at one time using wild cards, and script files to automate whole communication sessions. For information about Kermit, contact

Kermit Distribution

Columbia University Center for Computing Activities

612 West 115th Street

New York, NY 10025

You may also like to refer to the book *KERMIT: A File Transfer Protocol*, by Frank da Cruz (Bedford, Mass.: Digital Press, 1987).

USING A COMMERCIAL PROGRAM

Several commercial programs are available that enable UNIX users to connect to other UNIX or non-UNIX systems. One of these is Professional YAM. The name, standing for Yet Another Modem program, indicates its true UNIX origins. YAM offers a script language, enabling you to automate complete communications sessions; file transfer using a variety of protocols such as XMODEM, Kermit, and CompuServe's; and emulation of several standard terminals. YAM is available from

Omen Technology, Inc.

Box 4681

Portland, OR 97208

phone (503) 621-3406

My own program, XN/2392, will be of interest to those connecting to Hewlett-Packard computers. It emulates the HP2392A terminal on SCO XENIX and UNIX systems, and incorporates a script language and binary file transfer between HP3000 and UNIX systems. XN/2392 is available from

Minisoft, Inc.

16315 NE 87th Street, Suite B101

Redmond, WA 98052

phone (206) 883-1353

PART THREE

UNIX Communications for System Administrators

In the first two parts of this book I have given a general introduction to serial communications, and have described some UNIX communications utilities that are available to the general UNIX user.

In Part III I will describe serial communications under UNIX from the point of view of the system administrator. The first three chapters will describe the technical aspects: device drivers, how serial ports can be used for logins, and how to set the communications parameters. I will then describe how to administer *mail* and *uucp*.

As with the utility programs described in Part II, the facilities provided for system administrators differ among the various versions of UNIX. However, the principles are the same, and you will probably find that most of what follows applies to the system you use.

12

Device Drivers
and Serial Ports

Device drivers are sections of code that are used by operating systems and application programs to control devices such as serial ports. They are written so as to provide a consistent programming interface. This means that a program does not need to know how a particular device works in order to control it. The program simply sends a request in a standard format to the device driver, and the device driver does the rest.

Device drivers are incorporated into the *kernel* of the operating system. This is the portion that is loaded into memory when you boot UNIX. When you first install UNIX, a special version of the kernel is created by the installation process, incorporating the device drivers that you need. When you change your configuration, for example by adding a new serial card, you may have to create a new version of the kernel. This is known as *relinking* the kernel. In order to do this, you must have device drivers available for the new hardware. Your operating system probably came with a set of drivers for common devices. For other devices, you may have to incorporate device drivers supplied by the manufacturer of the device. For this reason, you should take care before ordering hardware for your system to ensure that a device driver is available.

INSTRUCTIONS TO DEVICE DRIVERS

I will explain in Part IV of this book the specific programming commands used. However, it will be helpful if I introduce here the basic commands that a program might issue to a serial device:

open

This command instructs the operating system to locate the particular driver and open up the communications port. This may include asserting hardware handshaking signals and initiating certain parameters such as baud rate to default values. With some versions of UNIX, the open command may fail if the device driver is already in use by another process; with others, multiple processes can happily access the same device at the same time, with potentially chaotic results. I will explain in Chapter 15 ("How UUCP Works") how UUCP avoids this situation by using special locking files.

read

The read command enables a program to read data from a device. It is important to understand two factors here. Firstly, a read command may retrieve data character by character or line by line. As we will see, a device driver can be instructed to return each character received, or each line received. Serial device drivers have access to a mechanism known as the *line discipline*. With appropriate programs, the programmer can be saved some work if the line discipline takes care of characters such as backspaces and other edits, and the program only has to deal with complete lines. However, this is not appropriate for all programs, and sometimes the device driver will be instructed to return each character typed. The second important factor is that the device driver will not always return exactly what was received from the serial port. It can be instructed to manipulate data in certain ways, such as converting all characters to upper case, or appending a line-feed character after each carriage return. The reason for this is to take account of the special requirements of certain terminals and other serial devices.

write

The write command enables the programmer to cause data to be transmitted out of the serial port. As with the read command, the line discipline may intervene and wait for a complete line to be available before transmitting anything, to add line feeds after carriage returns, etc.

close

Finally, a device can be closed. This terminates a communications session and may result in the handshaking signals being lowered, and the device being made available to other processes.

CONFIGURING DEVICE DRIVERS

As we will see in the next two chapters, special configuration instructions can be sent to device drivers. In the case of serial devices, typical instructions might be to set the baud rate and type of handshaking to use. Unlike the open, read, write and close commands, which can only be used by programmers, the configuration commands can be given by the user or system administrator. This can be done in two ways: by entries in special files that specify the initial configuration for a particular port, and by the use of the stty command. These two methods are described in the next two chapters respectively.

SPECIAL FILES

Each device driver has one or more files known as *device files* associated with it. These device files are of a type known as *special files*. Special files contain pointers to the device drivers within the kernel, and are stored on your system in the directory /dev. Typical names for special files associated with device drivers for serial ports are /dev/tty1, /dev/tty2, and so on. There may be only one device driver to handle all the serial ports; for each port the special file points to the appropriate section of the driver to handle that port.

Special files can be recognized in a long directory listing resulting from the ls -l command. The first character of the permissions column will be either *c* or *b*. If it is *c*, the file relates to a *character device*, such as a serial port, that handles input and output as a stream of bytes. If it is *b*, the file relates to a *block device*, such as a disk drive, a device that handles input and output as a series of blocks of data.

The following is an entry in /dev for the device tty1a, which in SCO XENIX is equivalent to the DOS COM1 port.

```
crw-rw-rw-  1 bin    bin    5,   0 Oct 23 17:50 tty1a
```

As you can see, the first character in the entry is *c*, indicating a character device. The numbers 5 and 0 are known as the major and minor device numbers, and indicate where in the kernel the code that handles this port is located. The remaining entries are the same as those for regular files, with which I am sure you are familiar. Incidentally, you may see entries for more ports than you actually have. This may be because your version of UNIX supports multiple virtual terminals on the console. For example, with XENIX you can switch between virtual terminals by pressing Alt-F1, Alt-F2, and so on. Special files are provided to support these virtual terminals and are listed in /dev.

SERIAL DRIVERS
FOR XENIX AND SCO UNIX

If you are not using XENIX or SCO UNIX, this section will not apply to you. If you are using one of those systems, you may find what follows helpful.

The driver entries corresponding to the ports generally referred to on the IBM PC as COM1, COM2, and so on are called tty1a, tty2a, etc. If you have a dumb multiple-port expansion board installed with four ports sharing the address for COM1, the appropriate driver entries will be tty1a, tty1b, tty1c and tty1d. Similarly, ports sharing COM2 would be referred to as tty2a, tty2b, and so on.

There is also a set of driver entries called tty1A, tty2A, etc. Notice that the last character in the name is in upper case. As you know, UNIX file names are case sensitive, unlike those in DOS. You can address COM1, for example, by using either the driver entry tty1a or the driver tty1A. However, these drivers are not identical.

The driver entries with the last character in upper case (tty1A, tty2A, etc.) have what SCO calls "modem control." According to the XENIX manual, this means that they will not transmit unless an incoming signal is detected on pin 8 (CD, Carrier Detect). In fact, this is not strictly correct. If it were so, you could not use a modern auto-dial modem as it is intended to be used. These modems do not assert CD until a carrier is actually present—in other words, until you are connected to another computer. If the tty1A driver really would not transmit until CD were present you could never transmit to the modem an instruction to dial. I have found that the driver will in fact transmit even without CD, but that if CD is raised and then lowered it will cease to transmit.

The device driver entries that have the last character in lower case (tty1a, tty2a etc) ignore the CD signal; however, they do assert RTS and DTR, even though the XENIX manual says that they do not.

CHOICE OF DRIVER FOR DIAL-IN PORTS

When you configure a port for dial-in, meaning that the port is connected to a modem and that users can dial into the system via that modem, you should use the version with "modem control." A great advantage of this is that if the connection is lost for any reason the driver will recognize the loss of the CD signal and close the port. Without this safeguard, the next person to dial in would be connected to the same session, without having to give a name and password— an obvious security risk.

CHOICE OF DRIVER FOR DIAL-OUT PORTS

If you want to dial out via a port that is connected to a modem, you can use either the modem or the non-modem version of the driver.

CHOICE OF DRIVER FOR DIRECT CONNECTIONS

When you are directly connecting a serial port to a terminal or another computer, you should select the non-modem version of the driver, since the other device will not necessarily assert CD.

INTELLIGENT COMMUNICATIONS BOARDS

The short sections above apply to the device drivers provided by SCO and to standard "dumb" serial ports. Some of the more intelligent serial boards, such as those from DigiBoard, can handle more communications functions such as buffering and handshaking internally, thereby reducing the load on the CPU and increasing effective throughput. These "smart" boards come with their own device drivers that may be different from the standard SCO drivers described above.

SPECIFYING PORTS

Communications software, whether a standard UNIX utility such as UUCP and *cu* or a commercial applications program, must be configured so as to know which device driver to use. This can be done in two ways. Some software enables you to specify a device on the command line, and some software has a configuration option that saves the names of devices in a separate file.

SPECIFYING A PORT
ON THE COMMAND LINE

The first way is to give the name of the device file associated with a particular port on the command line. For example, you may recall that with the cu command described in Chapter 11 you can specify a particular device on the command line as in the following example:

    cu -l tty1a *phonenumber*

In this case, you are instructing *cu* to connect with the serial port tty1a.

CREATING A CONFIGURATION FILE

Other software has an installation option that saves a list of device files in a configuration file. For example, my own company has developed a program called XN/2392, an HP2392A terminal emulator for XENIX. When you install XN/2392, you must create an ASCII file called *devlist*. In that file, you list the names of the serial ports that you wish to use. When you run XN/2392, it reads devlist, and attempts to use the first serial port listed. If that port is already in use, XN/2392 proceeds to the next port listed and so on until it finds one that is available.

13

Configuring Ports
for Logins

If you want a user to be able to log in to your system via a terminal connected to a particular serial port, either directly or via modems, you need to set up that port to allow logins, and to specify a default baud rate and other settings. If you want to use a serial port to dial out to another computer, or to connect to a serial printer, you must disable logins.

In this Chapter I will start by describing how logins work in UNIX. I will then give the formats of the various files used during the login process, and show how you can modify these files to suit your own installation. I will conclude by describing the flags used to set up the initial parameters for a login port.

LOGINS IN UNIX

If communications is a black art, then the internal workings of UNIX are a mystical religion; this is why its practitioners are called gurus. I will try to avoid getting too technical, but some knowledge of the subject is necessary in order to understand how logins are handled.

PARENT AND CHILD PROCESSES

In UNIX, a process can start up another process in one of two ways. In the first way, known as *exec*, the first process terminates and the new process starts. In the second way, known as *spawn*, the old process remains until the new process terminates and then the old process takes over again. The second process can spawn a third, and so on. A process that spawns another is known as the *parent*, and the process that is spawned is known as the *child*. If a process is spawned and then spawns another process, it will be the child of one process and the parent of another. However, if process A spawns process B, and process B execs process C, rather than spawning it, process C will be the child of process A.

By using the command

ps -el

you can see a list of all the processes currently running on your system. Each process has a number, or PID (for process ID), and with each process you can see the ID of its parent (PPID, for parent's process ID).

THE init PROCESS

When you boot up UNIX, the kernel performs several start-up functions, and then spawns the process called *init*. If you examine the list of current processes using the **ps** command, you will always see *init* listed— it is the ultimate parent of all the processes you will see listed except *swapper*, which is the parent of *init*.

One of the most important functions of *init* is to enable people to log in. It does this by watching for activity on each line that you have enabled for logins. When activity is detected (in the case of modem lines, through seeing the Carrier Detect line go high), *init* spawns the program *getty* (for "get tty").

In order for *init* to know which ports will be used for logins, it reads a file. This file is /etc/ttys or /etc/inittab depending on your version of UNIX. I will describe these files later in this chapter.

THE getty PROCESS

When *init* spawns *getty* it passes to *getty* the following parameters:

- **the timeout** (how long to wait for a valid response before giving up)
- **the name of the device file** for the particular port that it found in /etc/ttys or /etc/inittab
- **the label,** or line mode, that it found in /etc/ttys or /etc/inittab

getty now reads a file called *gettydefs* in the /etc directory. gettydefs consists of a number of entries each starting with a label. *getty* looks for an entry beginning with the label passed to it by *init*.

getty sets up the initial parameters, and waits for input on the communications line. When activity is detected on a line, *getty* transmits the login prompt and spawns the *login* program. *login* then reads the response and prompts for a password. If *login* receives a valid user name and password, *getty* then sets up the final parameters and execs the *shell* program that issues the UNIX prompt and interacts with the user.

Sometimes *uugetty* is used rather than *getty*. *uugetty* works in a similar way, but allows the same port to be used for both dial-out and dial-in purposes. This is typically used for ports that are connected to modems.

ENDING A SESSION

When the user ends the session, the shell program will die. This will return control to *init*, which will then spawn *getty* again in order to allow another user to log in.

ENABLING LOGINS

SCO XENIX and SCO UNIX have two commands, enable and disable, that enable and disable logins for a particular port by modifying /etc/ttys or /etc/inittab, and telling *init* to reread these files. With other versions of UNIX you may need to edit the file /etc/ttys or /etc/inittab in order to do this, and signal *init* that a change has been made.

FORMATS OF FILES USED IN THE LOGIN PROCESS

I have mentioned above three files that are used to control logins: /etc/ttys, /etc/inittab, and /etc/gettydefs. I will describe the format of these files and explain the fields that they contain.

THE ttys FILE

XENIX (and several other versions of UNIX) maintains a file called */etc/ttys* that lists the serial devices available and specifies whether a login is allowed.

The format of the /etc/ttys file is shown in Figure 13.1.

As you can see, each line has three entries: a *state flag* (1 if logins are permitted, 0 if not), a *line mode* that forms a key into the file /etc/gettydefs, and the name of a *device file* in the directory /dev.

The following is a sample entry in /etc/ttys:

    1dtty1a

The *1* indicates that logins are allowed on this device. The *d* means that *getty* should look for a line in /etc/gettydefs starting with *d* to find further instructions. The *tty1a* means that the device file to use is /dev/tty1a.

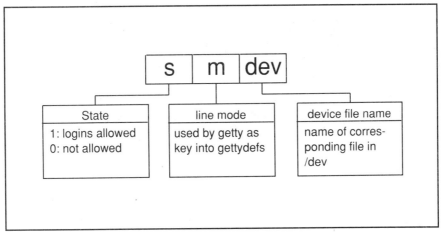

Figure 13.1: Format of the /etc/ttys file

THE inittab FILE

SCO UNIX, and other versions of UNIX System V, use a rather more complex method to control logins. Instead of /etc/ttys, they use /etc/inittab, which is used for other purposes than just logins. We will not be concerned here with these other purposes. The format of inittab is shown in Figure 13.2.

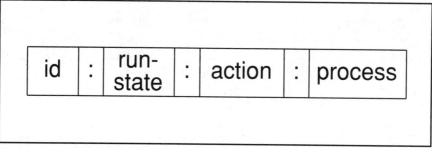

Figure 13.2: Format of the /etc/inittab file

As you can see, each line of inittab has four fields: *identifier*, *run-state*, *action*, and *process*. The fields are separated by the # sign and there is a blank line after each entry.

- **The identifier** is a key to identify the line.

- **The run-state** is a number indicating a *run level* at which the line will be executed, typically 2 for logins other than the first login on the console. If the current run level is lower than the number, *init* will skip the line. For example, if UNIX is currently in single-user mode, as it may be sometimes for system administration purposes, the run level might be 1 and any lines with a run-state higher than 1 (for example, lines permitting logins other than on the console) would be ignored.

- **The process** is the process to run. In the case of lines used for logins, this process would be *getty*. The process is followed by the arguments to pass to it. In the case of *getty*, these are timeout, the name of the device file, and a line mode, which is a key to an entry in /etc/gettydefs.

- **The action** can be one of a number of words, indicating, for example, that the process is only to be run once. In the case of logins, the action will be "respawn." This means that *init* is to run the process (*getty*), and, when it terminates (because the user logged off), run it again so that another user can log in.

THE gettydefs FILE

The gettydefs file is used by *getty* to determine various communications and other parameters. When *init* spawns *getty*, it passes a key word sometimes referred to as the line mode. *getty* reads through gettydefs until it finds a line starting with the key word that *init* passed to it. The key word is often, but not always, a representation of the baud rate (e.g., 9600). However, it is not interpreted in any way: in theory you could have a key word of 9600 to an entry in gettydefs that specified 1200 baud. Figure 13.3 shows the format of an entry in gettydefs.

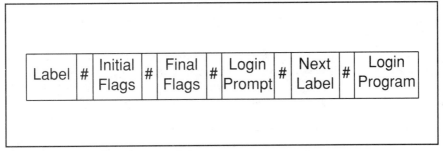

Figure 13.3: Format of a gettydefs entry

Each entry consists of the following fields, separated by a # sign:

label	The key by which *getty* finds the entry to use
initial flags	The baud rate and certain optional parameters to set before running the login program
final flags	The parameters to set after running the login program
login prompt	A prompt such as "Please login:"

next label   The label of the entry to jump to if a break signal is received

login program   This is an optional field used to specify a special login program other than the usual */etc/login*

Sometimes a user may try to log in at a different baud rate from the rate *getty* had set for that line. With some UNIX systems a user may request *getty* to try a different baud rate by pressing the Break key. This transmits a special signal that we described in Chapter 2. When *getty* receives a break signal, it will switch to another entry in gettydefs and follow the instructions there. Each entry in gettydefs ends with the key word for the next line to try when a break is received. If you want *getty* to ignore breaks then simply have the key word for the next entry to try be the same as the key word for the entry itself, so that *getty* will simply repeat the login process.

The following example shows three gettydefs entries that form a chain. The first specifies 2400 baud. If the user presses the break key, *getty* will jump to the entry that specifies 1200 baud. If another break signal is received, *getty* will jump to the entry for 300 baud, and on a third break it will jump back to the original entry.

```
2400 # B2400 SANE # B2400 SANE # Please login: # 1200

1200 # B1200 SANE # B1200 SANE # Please login: # 300

300  # B300  SANE # B300  SANE # Please login: # 2400
```

I have simplified the above example by including only one initial flag and one final flag. The flag SANE is an abbreviation for certain common options and will be explained later.

SETTING
PARAMETERS IN gettydefs

Each entry in gettydefs contains initial flags and final flags. These flags determine

- hardware communications parameters such as baud rate

- how the data is to be buffered

- translations of certain characters

- how to handle special characters and other signals

There are a great number of different flags; you will find them listed under *termio* in your system's documentation. Many of them are obsolete, and I will not give a complete list here. I will deal with the more commonly used flags in each category.

HARDWARE COMMUNICATIONS PARAMETERS

In Chapter 1 I described the various hardware parameters relating to serial communications. By setting appropriate flags in gettydefs, you can specify the baud rate and other parameters as follows:

Baud Rate

You can set all the standard baud rates in gettydefs by using a flag consisting of *B* followed by the baud rate. The following are the flags for the most common baud rates:

B300	300 baud
B1200	1200 baud
B2400	1200 baud
B9600	9600 baud

Some systems, such as SCO UNIX, allow you to set higher baud rates by using the flags B19200 and B38400. Some systems, such as SCO XENIX, use the flags EXTA and EXTB for these rates. EXTA and EXTB were originally used for serial devices that used an external clock to determine baud rate.

Word Length

You can set the number of data bits in a word anywhere between 5 and 8. The flags are

CS5	5-bit words
CS6	6-bit words
CS7	7-bit words
CS8	8-bit words

Stop Bits

If you want two stop bits to be used, set the flag CSTOPB. If CSTOPB is not set, one stop bit will be assumed.

Parity

The following flags are available to determine parity:

PARENB	Enable parity
PARODD	Set odd parity

If PARENB is not set, parity will not be used. If PARENB is set and PARODD is not set, even parity will be assumed.

Handshaking

You can set the type of hardware handshaking by using the CLOCAL flag. If you set CLOCAL, the system will assume a direct connection, and ignore incoming handshaking signals. However, it will assert DTR and RTS for the benefit of a connected device that requires these signals. If CLOCAL is not set, the system will assume that a modem is in use and require Carrier Detect to be present before communicating. This approach pre-dates modern auto-dial modems that you must instruct to dial before the carrier signal is received. Remember that SCO UNIX and XENIX use separate special files to configure the driver for modem and non-modem connections.

OTHER FLAGS

As I mentioned above, there are many other flags that can be used in /etc/gettydefs. However, many of them are obsolete. Furthermore, you only need to set the flags in gettydefs that are necessary to enable login to take place. Once the user has logged in, the parameters can be changed by using the stty command that is described in the next chapter, and set to the most appropriate configuration for that user and/or terminal type. I will therefore list here only the flags that are likely to be used.

HUPCL

The HUPCL flag is used often. It stands for Hang Up on Close. This is generally used for dial-in ports. When HUPCL is set, the device driver will hang up the line by lowering DTR when the last process associated with that line terminates, generally when a user logs off. It is a good idea to set HUPCL since users do not always remember to hang up the phone at the end of a session.

SANE

The SANE flag sets a number of flags to reasonable values. It is useful to restore sanity when another process may have set the device driver to an unusual configuration.

IXON AND IXOFF

The flags IXON and IXOFF are used to support the XON/XOFF method of handshaking. If IXON is set, the device driver will suspend transmissions to the terminal when it receives an XOFF signal, and resume them when it receives an XON signal. The IXOFF flag indicates that the driver can send an XOFF signal to the terminal to suspend its output, and an XON signal to resume.

Remember that gettydefs governs the communications settings prior to the execution of the user's shell. The presumption is that at this time you don't know what kind of terminal is being used. Since the terminal, or perhaps an intermediate device such as a multiplexer, might be using XON/XOFF, it is a good idea to include IXON in gettydefs. IXOFF should not generally be used, since you cannot know whether a calling device supports XON/XOFF and will react to those signals. The exception would be in cases where you have standardized on certain equipment and you know that XON/XOFF will always be available; even then, however, it is unlikely that a user will fill your input buffer in the course of responding to a login request.

SUMMARY

In this chapter I've described UNIX device drivers and special files, how individual ports are selected, and how you can configure a port so as to enable or disable logins.

In the next chapter, I will describe how you can configure serial ports using the stty command.

14

Configuring Ports

with *stty*

In the last Chapter I explained how you can configure ports for logins, including how you can set up the initial communications parameters.

Another way you can set up the parameters for a port is with the stty command. Although the options available with stty are similar to those available in the gettydefs file, you can use stty in more situations. In particular, you can use stty in situations where getty is not called—for example, in handling serial printers. Secondly, you can use stty during the course of a communications session.

You can only use stty to control a port that is already open. If you are the superuser, you can use stty to alter the settings for any current communications session; otherwise you can affect only your own current session (i.e., the settings for the port to which your terminal is currently connected). Once a port is closed, the settings will revert to their default values.

There are two versions of the stty command; the version you have depends on your version of UNIX. With System V systems, the format is

    stty *[p]* *[< device]*

With Berkeley UNIX and SCO XENIX, the format is

    stty *[p]* *[> device]*

I will use the second format for the examples in this chapter, but remember that your system may be different. In both cases, *p* is a parameter and *device* is a device file. If you omit *device*, the parameters for your current standard input device (the device with which you logged on) will be set. You can set multiple parameters in one line by simply adding them as in the following example:

    stty 1200 parodd > /dev/tty1

Here both 1200 baud and odd parity are set.

SETTING
COMMUNICATIONS PARAMETERS

In Part I of this book, I described various communications parameters that two devices need to agree upon before they can communicate serially. These are baud rate, parity, word length, and number of stop bits. In UNIX, you can set these parameters for a given device by using the stty command. Programmers can also set them through software by using system calls that I will describe in Part IV. Some software, such as the XN/2392 program mentioned in the last chapter, will set the parameters for you. However, for some purposes, you will need to set the parameters directly, especially when you set up ports that will be used to enable external terminals to log in to the system. The settings you configure with stty will be forgotten when you shut down the system; for this reason you will probably want to include some appropriate stty commands for your login ports in a file that is executed when you boot UNIX.

BAUD RATE

You can set the baud rate for a device using the stty command with the name of the device file and the baud rate. For example

    stty 1200 > /dev/tty1

sets the device tty1 to 1200 baud.

PARITY AND WORD LENGTH

The following options are available to set the parity you require:

stty parenb > *device*	Enable parity generation and checking
stty -parenb > *device*	Disable parity generation and checking
stty parodd > *device*	Set odd parity
stty -parodd > *device*	Set even parity

You may need to set a particular parity in order to conform to the requirements of an external device, but may want to ignore any parity errors. The following commands enable and disable parity checking:

stty inpck > *device*	Enable input parity checking
stty -inpck > *device*	Disable input parity checking
stty ignpar > *device*	Ignore any parity errors
stty -ignpar > *device*	Do not ignore parity errors
stty parmrk > *device*	Mark (display) parity errors
stty -parmrk > *device*	Do not mark parity errors

In order to set word length, you use the *cs* (character size) option. You can set 5, 6, 7, or 8-bit words. For example, to set a word length of 8, enter

stty cs8 > *device*

If you are receiving 8-bit words but want to ignore the eight bit, you can have the eight bit stripped by using the *istrip* parameter.

Table 14.1 shows the options that set both parity and word length in a single command.

STOP BITS

You can set the number of stop bits by using the *cstopb* parameter. To

Table 14.1: stty Options for Setting Both Parity and Word Length

Command	Parity	Data Bits
stty evenp > *device*	even	7
stty oddp > *device*	odd	7
stty -evenp > *device*	none	8
stty -oddp > *device*	none	8
stty parity > *device*	enabled	7
stty -parity > *device*	none	8

set two stop bits, enter

> stty cstopb > *device*

To set one stop bit, enter

> stty -cstopb > *device*

DUPLEX

You can request the device driver to echo back characters received from the remote device (full duplex) by using the *echo* parameter. To disable echoing (half duplex) enter

> stty -echo > *device*

HANDSHAKING

I described both hardware and software handshaking in Part I of this book. The following parameters can enable both of these:

ctsflow   Enable CTS handshaking. The computer will not transmit to the device unless the CTS line is high

-ctsflow   Disable CTS handshaking

rtsflow   Enable RTS handshaking. The computer will lower the RTS line when it is not ready to receive data from the device

-rtsflow   Disable RTS handshaking

ixon   Obey XON/XOFF signals from the external device. Stop transmitting when XOFF is received, resume when XON is received

-ixon   Disregard XON/XOFF signals from the external device ixany   Resume transmitting when any character is received from the external device

ixoff   Send an XOFF signal to the remote device when the input queue is almost full. Send an XON signal when ready to receive more input

-ixoff   Do not transmit XON/XOFF signals

I personally find these quite confusing—who would have guessed that *ixon* related to both XON and XOFF signals received, and that *ixoff* related to both XON and XOFF signals transmitted? I hope that the above table will help with what must be one of the more perverse UNIX options.

CHARACTER PROCESSING

With the stty command, you can also instruct the device driver to process in certain ways characters that are transmitted and received. For example, you could instruct the driver to add an extra line feed after each carriage return that is transmitted, to allow for devices such as certain printers that require this. You can also tell the driver to insert delays after certain characters in order to give very slow devices time to react. Finally, you can instruct the driver how to handle certain special characters such as an interrupt or a break signal.

CARRIAGE RETURNS AND LINE FEEDS

The following parameters affect how the device driver will handle received and transmitted carriage returns and line feeds:

inlcr   Change received new-line character (ASCII 10) to a carriage return (ASCII 13)

igncr   Ignore received carriage returns

icrnl   Change received carriage-return characters to new-line characters

onlcr   Change transmitted new-line characters to carriage-
         return characters

ocrnl   Change transmitted carriage-return characters to new-
         line characters

onocr   Do not transmit a carriage return if the cursor is already
         at column zero (left hand edge of the screen)

onlret   Assume that the device itself will do a carriage return
         when it receives a new-line character

nl   Set *icrnl* and *onlcr* (see above).

All the above parameters can be cancelled by preceding them with a
minus sign. For example

stty -inlcr > /dev/tty

cancels the mapping of new-line characters to carriage-return characters.

DELAYS

Certain parameters instruct the device driver to insert delays after certain characters. They are primarily used to handle ancient printers that
have no buffers and may need time to perform a physical carriage return
before receiving the next character. I will not deal with these here; if you
need to use them you will find details in the UNIX documentation.

INTERRUPTS

When the connected device is a terminal, you will probably want to
enable the user to use the INTERRUPT and QUIT keys. By default, the
driver will generate a special signal to the operating system when one of
these characters is received. This is often necessary in order to abort a
UNIX application. The parameter *isig* instructs the device driver to do this.

However, if the device is another computer with which you are ex-
changing binary data, you would not want a signal to be generated when
the binary data happen to include an interrupt character. To prevent this,

you can use the parameter *-isig*. If you are using commercial applications software to handle the communications, the software may take care of this setting for you.

You can also arrange for the driver to issue the interrupt signal when a break signal is received on the line. I described the break signal in Chapter 2. If you want the break to trigger an interrupt, use the *brkint* parameter. You must also ensure that *ignbrk* (ignore break) is not set. The following example ensures that a break signal will generate an interrupt

```
stty -ignbrk brkint > /dev/tty1
```

To cancel this setting, use the parameter *-brkint* or *ignbrk*.

HANG-UP

Sometimes you may want to give a device driver a direct command to hang up the phone line. It does this by lowering the DTR signal to the modem; most modems will drop the connection when DTR is lowered. For example, if you have a modem attached to the port controlled by /dev/tty1, you can hang up the line by typing

```
stty 0 > /dev/tty1
```

You will generally want the device driver to hang up the phone line automatically when the last job associated with that line terminates. This will normally be when a dial-in user terminates the session. Users will normally disconnect the line themselves, but they sometimes forget and it is helpful to instruct the driver to hang up automatically. To do this, enter

```
stty hupcl > /dev/tty1
```

OTHER stty OPTIONS

Some of the parameters to the stty command are rarely used, and need not be described in detail here. The general categories they fall into are as follows:

- **case conversion** Some obsolete terminals could only handle upper-case characters. If you need to convert characters for a terminal from lower case to upper case and vice versa, refer to the parameters *xcase*, *lcase*, *iuclc*, and *olcuc* in your manual.

• **synchronous lines** If you are using a synchronous communications line, refer to the parameters *stwrap*, *stflush*, and *stappl*.

KEEPING PORT SETTINGS ALIVE

As I mentioned at the start of this chapter, stty affects only open ports. When a port is closed, its settings revert to default values. This is not generally a problem; we can configure the system so that *getty* and *uugetty* set up appropriate values whenever a port is opened. However, you sometimes want to set up special default values for a port that is connected, for example, to a serial printer. In order to do this, you can set up a background task that continually loops, resetting the values for a particular port to those that you want. For example, to keep port tty1a at 1200 bps you could use the following command:

```
(stty 1200; while: ; do sleep 3600; done) > /dev/tty1a &
```

This command operates in the background (note the ampersand at the end of the line) to keep the port at the settings you want. You can have this script run automatically when your system starts up, by including it in an *rc* file; see the documentation for your system for how to do this.

15

How *UUCP* Works

In Chapter 10, I introduced the Honey DanBer UUCP package and described the programs that form part of that package and are available for the general UNIX user. In this and the next two chapters I will explain UUCP in greater detail. In this chapter, I will explain how UUCP works, and describe the files that it uses. In Chapter 16, I will explain how to configure UUCP, including how to record details of the sites that you will be calling or that will be calling you. In Chapter 17, I will describe the various utility programs that form part of the UUCP package, and give some hints on troubleshooting.

Within this chapter, I will assume for simplicity that the remote site is accessed by telephone, and I will refer to the procedures in terms of dialing a site. However, UUCP can equally be used to transfer files to other systems that are directly connected, as we will see in the next chapter.

BASIC UUCP OPERATION

The following is the typical sequence of events governing a UUCP file transfer:

1. A user requests the file transfer, using uucp or mail.

2. *uucp* places a copy of the file to be transferred, or its path name, and instructions for transmitting the file in a special directory maintained for the target site.

3. *uucp* invokes *uucico*, which is a program that actually makes connections with remote sites. *uucico* examines the instructions that you have recorded for the particular target site, to see whether a connection may be attempted. If the target is a site that can be called, and the current time is within the time limits for calling that site, then *uucico* attempts to call the target site, make the connection, and transfer the file. At the same time, it will transfer any other outstanding files for that site, and receive any files that the remote site has for our site.

In addition to the above procedure, triggered each time a user requests a file transfer, there is a set of procedures that govern scheduled connections. At specified times, UUCP looks to see what transfers are pending, and checks to see which of them may be attempted at the current time. This takes care of transferring files to sites that can be called only within certain times, and reattempting connections that failed for one reason or other when they were initially attempted. You can also set up UUCP to call, or *poll*, certain sites at regular times even if there are no files for them, to check to see whether those sites have messages for you; this is only necessary for sites that you can call but that cannot call you.

There are therefore four basic possibilities for a file transfer:

- UUCP immediately dials the site and requests a connection.
- UUCP waits until a specified time and then dials the site and requests a connection.
- UUCP waits for the site to dial your machine, and then initiates the transfer.
- While UUCP is waiting for the time to dial the site, the site dials into your system. UUCP then transfers the file.

UUCP CONNECTIONS

When one UUCP site dials another, it is initially seen as just another user logging in. When you arrange with the system administrator of a site to set up dial-up facilities for your machine, you will be given a login name and password for UUCP to use. When you set up that site in your system as a site that UUCP can dial, you record the name and password. You also record other information such as baud rate and time of day to dial.

Once your copy of UUCP has successfully logged in to another system, it can request programs to be run on that system. However, for security reasons the programs that can be run by an external UUCP system are generally severely restricted. I will explain later in this chapter how this happens. This is why I mentioned in Chapter 10 that the *uux* program to execute a program on a remote system cannot be relied upon to work. However, permission will be given to run the program *rmail* (receive mail).

This program enables your copy of UUCP to transmit messages to an individual user on the remote system.

The following is a typical sequence of events in a UUCP transfer.

1. The UUCP program *uucico* on system A dials up system B, and logs in by responding with an agreed login name and password.

2. System B runs its own copy of *uucico*, as the shell for the copy of *uucico* that has logged in.

3. The two copies of *uucico* agree on a communications protocol to use; this is generally the /g protocol.

3. System A passes to system B a series of requests, which are generally requests to run *rmail* (receive mail) to transfer messages to users on system B.

4. If system B has messages for system A, system B likewise transfers a series of requests.

5. System A checks again to see whether any further messages have been spooled for system B during stages 1 through 4. If there are more messages, stages 3 and 4 are repeated until neither system has any pending messages.

6. System A logs off from system B.

7. System A and system B each run the program *uuxqt* that processes the requests received from each other.

UUCP SCHEDULING

I mentioned earlier in this chapter that UUCP incorporates a scheduling system that takes care of any transfers that cannot take place immediately. The scheduling system is governed by the UNIX *cron* program.

cron

If you are familiar with the UNIX *cron* program you may skip this section. *cron* runs continually in the background on UNIX systems, taking care of regularly scheduled events. *cron* is driven by files contained in the directory /usr/spool/cron/crontabs. These files each have the name of the user that set them up. For example, the activities specified by the user *root* are contained in the file /usr/spool/cron/crontabs/root.

Each crontabs file consists of a list of entries; each entry consists of six fields:

- minute
- hour (1 through 24)
- day of month
- month
- day of week
- command

Each of the time fields can contain an asterisk or a number. The asterisk instructs UUCP to execute the command every minute, every hour, or whatever, according to the field indicated. For example,

    10 * * * * *command*

means execute the specified command at ten minutes after every hour, every day of the year, and

    30 9 * * * *command*

means execute the command at thirty minutes past nine every day. Entries can also contain commas to indicate more than one time in the same field, and hyphens to indicate ranges. For example

    10,40 * * * * *command*

means execute the command at both 10 minutes and 40 minutes after each hour, and

    0 14 * * * 1-5

means execute the command at exactly 2 p.m. on weekdays (Monday through Friday).

The regularly scheduled activities for UUCP are specified in a crontabs file in the above format. They are generally contained either in the crontabs file for root, or in a separate crontabs file for the *uucp* account. The activities consist of UUCP programs and script files as discussed in the following sections.

uudemon.hour

The first program that should be run regularly through *cron* is *uudemon.hour*. This is a script file that executes two UUCP programs: *uusched* and *uuxqt*. The first of these, *uusched*, searches through the subdirectories for each site under the directory /usr/spool/uucp to see whether there are any pending transfers. *uusched* then invokes *uucico* for each site for which there is work—in random order. The connections can then be made and transfers undertaken. *uudemon.hour* then executes *uuxqt*, which searches for and executes command files that have been received from remote systems and not yet executed.

Despite its name, *uudemon.hour* is often run more than once an hour, especially where sites do not want to have to wait an hour for a failed connection to be reattempted. The following crontabs entry runs it at both 10 and 40 minutes past the hour:

```
10,40 * * * * /bin/su uucp -c "/usr/lib/uucp/uudemon.hour" > /dev/null
```

TIP

The sample crontabs file supplied with SCO XENIX runs *uudemon.hour* at 9 minutes and 39 minutes past each hour. Imagine tens of thousands of machines all trying to connect at exactly those times. You might expect a large number of failed calls due to busy signals. I recommend that you do not use these particular times in your installation.

---

uudemon.poll

The next script that is regularly run from *cron* is *uudemon.poll*. This script is usually run once an hour, and reads the file /usr/lib/uucp/Poll to see whether any sites are due to be polled during that particular hour.

Recall that polling is used for sites that do not call your own site, to see whether they have any messages for your site. *uudemon.poll* works by creating dummy work files for each site to be polled. It should be run before *uudemon.hour*, which runs *uusched*, which in turn sees the dummy work files created by *uudemon.poll* and instructs *uucico* to call the sites.

uudemon.admin

The next script file that is run regularly is *uudemon.admin*. This script file runs the UUCP program *uustat*, which reports on the current status of UUCP activity. I will describe *uustat* in full in Chapter 17 ("UUCP Utility Programs and Troubleshooting"). The script also checks for current activity by looking at the lock files described later in this chapter. *uudemon.admin* sends these reports by mail to the login account for UUCP. In order to read these messages, log in as "root" and type

```
mail -u uucp
```

Do not attempt to log in as uucp; this login account is intended for logins from remote systems and runs *uucico* automatically.

uudemon.clean

The last of the four regularly executed scripts is *uudemon.clean*. This script makes backup copies of a number of internal UUCP files, and then executes *uuclean*, which is a program that "cleans up" your UUCP system by getting rid of old files. *uuclean* is described further in Chapter 17.

CONFIGURATION FILES

I will continue this explanation of how UUCP works by describing briefly each of the files that govern the operation of UUCP. These files are created and maintained by the system Administrator or through SCO's *uuinstall* program, and record the name of your site, information about remote sites and how to access them, and information about the devices that are available to make external connections. In the next chapter ("Configuring UUCP"), I will describe the files in far greater detail. The files are listd in Table 15.1.

Table 15.1: UUCP Configuration Files

Directory	File Name	Use
/etc	systemid	Contains the name of your own site. (Not used in all versions of UUCP)
/usr/lib/uucp	Systems	Entries for each site that you can connect to, with instructions on how and when to connect to it and how to log in
/usr/lib/uucp	Devices	A list of the devices (such as modems) that you can use to connect to other sites
/usr/lib/uucp	Dialers	A list of dialers, including auto-dial modems, and instructions on how to use them
/usr/lib/uucp	Permissions	Indicates for each remote site what that site is allowed to do on your own system
/usr/lib/uucp	Poll	Lists times to call each site that is to be called regularly

Note that the directories where these files are found may differ from system to system, but the above are the most common.

INTERNAL FILES

I will conclude my explanation of how UUCP works by describing the internal files that are created by UUCP itself in the course of its operation. (These are not the same files as those created by the administrator to control UUCP.)

DATA FILES

You will recall from Chapter 10 that with the uucp command you can request UUCP to transmit either a file or a copy of a file. The difference is that if you request a copy to be transmitted, and you change the file before the transmission takes place, the unchanged version will be transmitted. The copy is saved as a data file in the subdirectory for the target site under the directory /usr/spool/uucp. Data files have names starting with D. followed by an automatically generated extension.

CONTROL FILES

Each time you use the uucp or uux command, UUCP creates a control file. The control file is held in the subdirectory for the particular remote site, under the directory /usr/spool/uucp. Control file names start with C. followed by an extension. The extension contains an automatically generated sequential number (see the description of the .Sequence files below).

Control files can contain more than one entry, since a single uucp command can generate more than one request. Each entry consists of the following fields:

send/receive flag	*S* for Send, *R* for Receive
source	The pathname of the source file
destination	The pathname of the destination file
local user	The name of the user at the local site
directory flag	*d* = create directory, *-d* = do not create directory
copy flag	*c* = source is a copy, *-c* = not a copy
data file	The name of the data file (only used if the transaction is a send)
source mode	The file mode of the source file
notify	The name of the user to notify of problems
status file	The name of the file to which to report the transfer status. Null if no file was specified

Note that the data file field is only relevant if a copy of the source file (rather than the source file itself) is being transmitted. If there is no data file, a dummy file name is used, since it will be ignored by UUCP.

EXECUTE FILES

Execute files are files that contain requests received from remote sites to execute programs locally, i.e., those resulting from a remote user running *uux*. They have file names beginning with X. followed by an extension including an automatically generated number, and are held in the subdirectory for the remote site under the directory /usr/spool/uucp.

STATUS FILES

UUCP maintains a status file for each remote site in the directory /usr/spool/uucp/.Status. Each status file indicates the last contact attempt, and the result. The fields in a status file are as follows:

status code	Zero if the contact was successful; otherwise an error code is recorded
number of attempts	The number of times UUCP tried to make contact
time	The time of the last attempted contact, in UNIX format
retry time	The time to wait before the next retry (This time is automatically increased with each retry)
status	A text description such as "SUCCESSFUL" or "CALLER SCRIPT FAILED"
site	The name of the remote site

LOCK FILES

One of the strange quirks of UNIX is that with most versions more than one process can access a serial device at the same time. This means that two copies of *uucico*, running at the same time, could simultaneously send data to the same port, with the result that the two transmissions would be mixed together.

In order to prevent this, when UUCP opens a particular port it creates a temporary file known as a *lock file*. Lock files are held in the directory /usr/spool/uucp. The file name is made up of the sequence LCK.. followed by the name of the device. For example, the lock file for the port *tty1a* would be /usr/spool/uucp/LCK..tty1a. The only data contained in a lock file is the process-ID of the process that created the lock.

When UUCP has finished with the device, it deletes the lock file, enabling other processes to access the port.

NOTE

If your system crashes during a *uucico* transfer, some lock files might be left undeleted. You may need to delete them manually before UUCP can access the relevant devices again.

Not all UNIX communications software checks for the existence of UUCP lock files. You might find that a non-UUCP process interrupts a *uucico* session by accessing the same port. If this is a problem at your site, you might want to write a script file that tests for the existence of a lock file, only runs the application if the file does not exist, and creates a lock file to prevent UUCP from interrupting the session.

xferstats

UUCP maintains a log of all file transfers in the file /usr/spool/uucp/.Admin/xferstats. The file contains one entry for each transfer, giving the site, date and time, device, time taken, and number of bytes transferred.

THE .Sequence DIRECTORY

You will recall that control files, data files, and execute files all have file extensions that are generated automatically. The directory /usr/spool/uucp/.Sequence contains a file for each site, containing a single entry: the last sequence number used for that site.

THE .Xqtdir DIRECTORY

The directory /usr/spool/uucp/.Xqtdir is the directory in which commands issued by a remote system are executed.

THE .Workspace DIRECTORY

The directory /usr/spool/uucp/.Workspace is used by UUCP to hold temporary files.

SUMMARY

In this chapter I have explained how UUCP works and described the files that it uses. In the next chapter I will describe the configuration files in greater detail, and how to maintain them.

16

Configuring *UUCP*

In the last chapter, I described how UUCP works, and mentioned the various configuration files that control its operation. These files are listed in Table 16.1. In this chapter I will describe the configuration files in greater detail, and explain how to maintain them.

Table 16.1: UUCP configuration files

DIRECTORY	FILE NAME	USE
/etc	systemid	Used by SCO versions of UNIX to record the name of your own site
/usr/lib/uucp	Systems	Entries for each site that you can connect to, with instructions on how and when to connect to it and how to log in
/usr/lib/uucp	Devices	A list of the devices such as modems that you can use to connect to other sites
/usr/lib/uucp	Dialers	A list of dialers, including auto-dial modems, and instructions on how to use them
/usr/lib/uucp	Permissions	Indicates for each remote site what that site is allowed to do on your own system
/usr/lib/uucp	Poll	Lists times to call each site that is to be called regularly

THE uuinstall PROGRAM

If you are using SCO XENIX or SCO UNIX, you can use the *uuinstall* program supplied with those systems. This is a menu-driven program that enables you to view and maintain most of these files very easily. I recommend that you at least start using UUCP by running *uuinstall*. However, *uuinstall* has some limitations: it does not maintain the Permissions, Dialers, or Poll files, and it does not make full use of the options available for scripting login sequences.

If you do not have access to *uuinstall*, you will have to maintain the files using a text editor. I will now describe each of the files in turn.

systemid

SCO XENIX and UNIX systems record the name of your site in the file /etc/systemid. They also record one or more machines named in this file for use by MICNET, an SCO networking system that is not covered in this book.

SYSTEMS

You can edit the Systems file directly, or use *uuinstall* if available. The file /usr/lib/uucp/Systems contains one entry for each remote site that you can call or that can call you. Each entry consists of the following fields, separated by spaces:

- site name
- time to call
- type of device to use
- baud rate
- phone number
- script for logging in

The format of these individual fields is described below:

SITE NAME

This is the name of the site with which you will be communicating. For example, if you want to send mail to sli!peterg, the site name is sli.

TIME TO CALL

You will have to agree with the administrator of the remote system about the times you will be able to call in. Some administrators will allow you to call at any time. In this case the time to call will read simply

Any

If this is the case, then whenever you request a UUCP transfer to that site (for example, via *mail*), UUCP will attempt to make the connection and transfer the file immediately.

Many system administrators will want to restrict UUCP logins to certain times, for example evenings and weekends, in order to cut down on the amount of activity during peak hours. You can enter one or more times to call a site. Each time consists of an indication of the day of the week, followed optionally by the start and end time. The day of the week is indicated by the first two letters, with the first letter capitalized. As an alternative to the day of the week, you can use "Any" to indicate any day, or "Wk" to indicate weekdays—i.e., Monday through Friday. The time or time range is shown in a 24-hour format. The following are some examples:

Any	Any day, any time
Any1800-2400	Any day between 6 p.m. and midnight
Mo0900-1200	Mondays between 9 a.m. and noon
SaSu	Saturdays and Sundays at any time
Wk1900-2030	Weekdays between 7 p.m. and 8:30 p.m.

SaSu,Wk1900-2000	Any time on Saturday or Sunday, and weekdays between 7 p.m. and 8 p.m.
Tu1900-0800	Between 7 p.m. Tuesday and 8 a.m. the next day (Wednesday)

Finally, for machines that call you rather than vice versa, you should enter the word "Never".

NOTE

Remember that setting the permissible times to call is not the same as instructing UUCP actually to call at those times.

DEVICE TYPE

This field is a key into the *Devices* file described later. It will normally be "ACU" for systems that you call by modem, or "Direct" for systems that are directly connected. Other device types can be added, as described later in the section entitled "The Devices File."

BAUD RATE

The baud rate is given as a fixed rate (e.g., 1200), a range (e.g., 1200-2400) or "Any ".

PHONE NUMBER

The phone-number field consists of a straight sequence of digits, without spaces or hyphens. For example

4081231234

The phone-number field can also contain an equals sign (=), telling

UUCP to wait for a second dial tone before continuing, or a hyphen, telling UUCP to pause four seconds. For example, the following sequence tells it to wait 4 seconds, dial 9, wait for a second dial tone, and dial 123-1234:

```
-9=1231234
```

UUCP will translate the hyphens and equals signs into the appropriate instructions for the modem in use.

Where the connection is via a data switch, the phone-number field can be used to indicate a token or sequence of characters used to select a particular connection.

Finally, the phone-number field can contain special abbreviations that you create and enter in the file /usr/lib/uucp/Dialcodes.

LOGIN SCRIPT

The remainder of the entry in the Systems file tells UUCP how to log in to the remote system. This consists of a series of exchanges, sometimes known as *chat scripts*. Each exchange consists of a prompt string that is *expected* to be received from the remote system, followed by the string to *send*. A simple example would be

```
Please log in: peterg
```

This instructs UUCP to wait for the string "Please log in", and reply *peterg*.

Several expect/send pairs can be combined in one line. For example, suppose that your UUCP login for a remote system is *uuslc* and your password was *secret*. You might want UUCP to wait for the string "please login:", reply *uuslc*, and then wait for the string "password" and reply *secret*. You do not need to enter the whole of the login prompts, just the last few characters. A sample login script could be as follows:

```
gin: uuslc word: secret
```

NOTE

Note that the commands are case-sensitive. If you tell UUCP to expect "Login" and it receives "login" it will ignore the string. This is why scripts often contain just "gin".

UUCP will always add a carriage return to strings to send, unless you add \c after the string. Use \r if you want to send just a carriage return. If you want UUCP to initiate the sequence—i.e., not to wait for an initial *expect* string—use " " as in the following example:

" ": \r gin: uuslc word: secret

This instructs UUCP to send an initial carriage return without waiting for anything; then wait for the string "gin:" and reply *uuslc*; then wait for "word:" and reply *secret*.

You can also specify *subexpect strings* and *subsend strings*. These pairs are separated by hyphens and contain alternatives to the main expect/send pair. They are in reverse order, with the string to send first. If the expect string is not received, UUCP sends the subsend string and waits for the subexpect string. For example,

gin-connect-gin uuslc

means Wait for the string "gin". If you receive it, reply *uuslc*; if you do not receive it, reply *connect*, wait for the string "gin", and then reply *uuslc*.

This explains the following cryptic but commonly used sequence:

gin--gin

This means Wait for the string "gin"; if you do not receive it, send a carriage return (i.e., a null string) and wait for the string "gin" again.

There are several special characters that you can use in chat scripts. Their meanings are as follows:

\N	An ASCII 0 (NUL)
\b	Backspace
\c	Suppress carriage return

\d	Wait two seconds
\p	Wait between ¼ second and ½ second
\E	Start echo-checking
\e	End echo-checking
\n	New-line character
\r	Carriage return
\s	Space
\t	Tab
\\	The backslash (\) character
EOT	ASCII 4 (EOT) plus new line plus ASCII 4 plus new line
BREAK	Break character
\K	Break character
xxx	ASCII character expressed in octal

Echo-checking means that UUCP is to wait for each character to be echoed from the remote system before sending a new one.

Special characters such as control characters can be expressed in octal. For example,

\003\r

means send Ctrl-C followed by a carriage return.

NOTE

The *cu* program described in Chapter 11 will read the Systems file to obtain dialing instructions for a site, but will not follow the chat script specified in Systems to log on. However, you can get *cu* to log on by creating a custom Dialer entry for that site that contains the appropriate expect-send pairs to log on once connection has been achieved. The Dialer file is described later in this chapter.

SAMPLE Systems ENTRY

The following example is a typical complete entry in the Systems file:

slc Any ACU 2400 4151231234 gin--gin: uuspl sword: Secret

This entry is for the remote site *slc*. It means that UUCP can dial slc at any time, use the entry in the Devices file marked *ACU*, and set a baud rate of 2400. The telephone number is 415 123 1234. The chat script waits for the sequence of characters *gin* (from the sequence "Please login") and replies with *uuspl*, your own site's login name for the site. It then waits for the sequence *sword* (from the sequence "Enter Password") and replies *Secret*.

THE Devices FILE

I mentioned in the last section that the entry in the Systems file for a particular site includes a reference to a device specified in the Devices file. This enables you to specify, for example, that a particular system is directly connected to the port /dev/tty6. Alternatively, you might specify that the site is to be called by a 2400-baud modem. In the file /usr/lib/uucp/Devices, you list the devices that are available for connecting with remote systems, and give further information about those devices.

The file /usr/lib/uucp/Devices contains one entry for each device. Each entry has the following fields:

type	A key name such as ACU that is specified as the device for a site in the Systems file. UUCP looks in Devices for a device with that type
tty	The name of the port for the device, for example /dev/tty1A
dialer	This is used for 801-type dialers that are separate from modems. If an 801-type dialer is not in use, as is usually the case, enter a hyphen

| speed | The baud rate or range of baud rates for that device |
| dialer-token | The name of a dialer program or a key into the Dialers file, and a token string to pass to the dialer program or to use in connection with the entry in the Dialers file. |

TYPE

Note that there can be more than one device with the same type. When UUCP wants to connect to a particular site, it looks in the Systems file for the device type and speed specified for that site. It then looks in the Devices file for a device having that type and speed. If the first matching device is not available, UUCP continues to look through the Devices file for another device that matches the specified type and speed, and so on until it either finds an available device or reaches the end of the file.

DIALER-TOKEN PAIRS

The dialer can be one of the following:

- a special program, such as those provided by SCO to control Hayes-compatible modems

- a key to an entry in the Dialers file described below

- the word *direct*, indicating a direct connection

If the dialer begins with a forward slash (/), or if a file is found in /usr/lib/uucp with the same name, it will be treated as a program; otherwise it will be treated as a key into Dialers.

The *token* is a string of characters to pass to the dialer program or to be processed according to the entry in Dialers. If the token is blank, the phone-number entry from Systems will be passed instead. The token can also contain the special code /T, meaning translate the phone-number according to the translation tables contained in the file Dialcodes described below, or /D, meaning do not translate the phone number but pass it through unmodified.

If there is more than one dialer-token pair, UUCP will use the second pair if the first one fails.

SAMPLE Devices ENTRY

The following is a sample entry from the Devices file:

ACU /dev/tty1A - 2400 /usr/lib/uucp/hayes24 /D

This entry means that where ACU is specified in Systems as the device for a particular site, use the port /dev/tty1A at a baud rate of 2400. Use the special program /usr/lib/uucp/hayes24 rather than following the instructions in the Dialers file, and pass the telephone number for the site from Systems through to the dialer program without translating the number.

THE Dialers FILE

The file /usr/lib/uucp/Dialers is used to tell UUCP how to use the various auto-dial modems or other dialers that you may have. This is needed because although the Hayes AT command set described in Chapter 4 is widely used, some modems and dialers use different commands. The Dialers file contains a list of entries, with one entry for each dialer.

The first field in each entry is the dialer name. This is the key used in the Devices file to specify a particular dialer.

After the dialer name comes a list of substitutions. This list consists of pairs of characters; UUCP uses the list to translate special characters used in the dialing instructions into the characters appropriate for that dialer. For example, the Hayes modems use a comma to indicate a pause; UUCP uses a hyphen for a pause. The Dialers entry for Hayes modems therefore contains the character pair

-,

meaning "change all hyphens to commas before passing the string to the dialer."

After the substitution list comes a script indicating how to instruct the dialer to dial. The script consists of successive pairs of strings to expect and to send, in the same format as that used for login instructions in the Systems file described earlier in this chapter. For example, with Hayes modems the instructions to dial might be to transmit AT followed by a carriage return, wait for the modem to respond OK, transmit ATDT followed by the phone number and a carriage return, and wait for the modem to respond CONNECT. You can use the same special symbols described above under the Systems file.

THE Dialcodes FILE

The file /usr/lib/uucp/Dialcodes can be used to hold abbreviations that you can use in the phone-number field of the Systems file. Entries are in pairs consisting of the abbreviation and the expansion. For example, if you had the following entry in Dialcodes—

    London 9=0101441

—then you could enter a phone number in Systems as

    London 1231234

UUCP would then dial 9, wait for a second dial tone, and then dial 01014411231234.

THE Permissions FILE

Imagine that a caller dialing into your system had unrestricted rights to execute commands on your system. He or she could read your private mail, delete files, and cause all sorts of havoc. UUCP has several safety precautions built into it to prevent this; they will help to protect your site, but bear in mind that they are not considered sufficient for protecting sensitive government information. I am told that sites with classified information stored on their systems are not allowed to use UUCP at all.

The file /usr/lib/uucp/Permissions contains one entry for each remote site. Each entry specifies what that site is allowed to do with respect to your own site: what programs it can run, whether it can request files, and so on.

The Permissions file has a different format from the other files we have discussed in this chapter. As before, each entry consists of a single logical line, extended with backslash characters (\) where it exceeds the maximum physical line length. However, each field in each entry consists of a field name followed by an equals sign and the field contents. For example,

    REQUEST=yes

In this example, the field name is REQUEST, and the field contents are "yes". Do not leave a space on either side of the equals sign.

THE SITE NAME

A connection with a remote computer can be initiated by your computer dialing out, or by the remote computer dialing in. If your computer dials another site called *slc*, you should have a Permissions entry for slc starting

    MACHINE=slc

If the slc site will be dialing in to your computer, and uses the login name *uuslc*, you should have a Permissions entry starting

    LOGNAME=uuslc

If sometimes your computer calls slc and sometimes slc calls your computer, you will need either a combined LOGNAME MACHINE entry or separate entries.

If you want to give the same permissions to more than one site, you can combine their entries in one. For example, to give the same permissions to slc and sco, start the entry with

    LOGNAME=slc:sco

You can also specify that a particular site have the same permissions whether it is dialing in or being dialed. You do this by combining an entry as follows:

LOGNAME=uuslc MACHINE=slc

You can also give the same login name to several different sites, and combine their LOGNAME permissions under an entry for that login name. When one of those sites dials in, UUCP will find out through the *uucico* exchange which site it is. You can limit the sites that can use a particular login name by using the VALIDATE command followed by a list of sites, for example:

LOGNAME=uuaccess VALIDATE=friend1: friend2: friend3

THE CALLBACK FIELD

You can gain considerable protection against attempted break-ins by using the optional CALLBACK field. Simply type CALLBACK under the entry for a site, and UUCP will not accept any instructions, but will call the site back after it calls you, before proceeding with file transfers and other business.

THE COMMANDS FIELD

The COMMANDS entry in Permissions indicates which commands the remote site may execute on your system. The COMMANDS field is only used on MACHINE entries, not on LOGNAME entries. However, the entry for a site under MACHINE will specify the commands that the site may issue regardless of whether it calls you or you call it.

After the COMMANDS key word and the equals sign, you list the programs that can be executed, separated by colons as in the following example:

COMMANDS=rmail:rnews:uucp

If the programs are not on the default path, you must give the full path with the program name. For example:

    COMMANDS=/usr/peterg/bin/sendit

You can also use ALL to indicate all available programs. If ALL is used without a path name, it indicates all the programs on the default path. You can also specify that all the commands in a particular directory can be executed, simply by listing that directory.

The following is a more complicated example:

    COMMANDS=ALL:/usr/peterg/bin:/usr/jimt/bin/doit

This entry enables the remote system to execute any command on the default path, any command in the directory /usr/peterg/bin, and the program *doit* in the directory /usr/jimt/bin.

You should take great care in setting up the permissions for a remote site. Allowing an outsider to execute commands on your system can allow access to confidential information or malicious destruction of your data.

THE REQUEST, READ, AND NOREAD FIELDS

Three fields—REQUEST, READ, and NOREAD—indicate which files the remote site can request your system to transmit. Together, they form an important part of your security system, since you will often want to protect confidential data.

If you do not want the remote site to be able to request any files, enter

    REQUEST=no

If you want the remote site to be able to read files only in the directory /usr/spool/uucppublic, enter

    REQUEST=yes

and do not use the READ or NOREAD fields.

If you want to specify exactly which files a remote system can access, use the READ commands. For example, to enable a remote system to request files from the directory /usr/pubinfo enter

REQUEST=yes

READ=/usr/pubinfo

This will allow access additionally to any subdirectories under the one specified. Suppose you wanted a remote site to be able to request any file on your system under the /usr directory except those in /usr/president/salaries. You could specify this with the following entries:

REQUEST=yes

READ=/usr

NOREAD=/usr/president/salaries

As you see, the READ field limits the REQUEST field, and the NOREAD field in turn limits the READ field.

THE WRITE AND NOWRITE FIELDS

The WRITE and NOWRITE fields are similar to the READ and NOREAD fields. If the WRITE field is not included, a remote site will only be able to write files to /usr/spool/uucppublic. With the WRITE field, you can extend the permission to write to particular directories, and with the NOWRITE field you can prevent a remote site from writing to specified directories. The following entries allow a site to write to all directories under /usr/peterg except /usr/peterg/private:

WRITE=/usr/peterg

NOWRITE=/usr/peterg/private

THE Poll FILE

The next configuration file is the file /usr/lib/uucp/Poll. This file contains instructions to UUCP to call certain sites at preset times to see whether they have any messages for your site. You do not need entries in Poll for sites that automatically call you when they have messages.

The format of the Poll file is very simple. Each entry starts with a site name. The site name is followed by a tab character, and then by a list of times to call. Each time is a number between 0 (midnight) and 23 (11 p.m.). A sample entry would be

    slc 8 14 22

This entry tells UUCP to call slc at 8 a.m., 2 p.m., and 10 p.m. each day.

NOTE

You might not want the calls to take place at the same time every day; for example, you might not want polling to take place on weekends, or you might want just one poll on Sundays. You can achieve this by creating more than one Poll file, such as Pollwk for weekdays and Pollwe for weekends. Then add a line to your crontabs file to copy Pollwk to Poll every Monday, and Pollwe to Poll every Saturday.

In order to see how the Poll file is used, look at the script file uudemon.poll in the directory /usr/lib/uucp.

THE remote.unknown FILE

Some sites publish general *uucp* logins so that anybody can dial in. When a site logs in with a valid login name and password, but indicates to *uucico* a site name that is not found in the Systems file, the script file remote.unknown is executed. If you do not want unknown sites to be able to connect, change the permissions settings on the file remote.unknown so that it cannot be executed.

THE Sysfiles FILE

The last configuration file is the optional file /usr/lib/uucp/Sysfiles. This file is used to specify alternative files to use instead of the files such as Systems and Dialers discussed above. For example, you could split your Systems file into three: Sys1, Sys2, and Sys3. In order to tell UUCP that you have done this, create a Sysfiles file with the following entry:

```
service=uucico:cu systems=Sys1:Sys2:Sys3
```

You could also specify different files for *uucico* and *cu*. For example, you could use the following entries:

```
service=uucico dialers=dialuu
service=cu dialers=dialcu
```

17

UUCP Utilities and
Troubleshooting

This is the last of four chapters on UUCP. In Chapter 9, I described UUCP from the user's point of view, and the UUCP programs and facilities available to users other than system administrators. In Chapter 15, I explained how UUCP works internally. In Chapter 16, I described how to configure UUCP. In this chapter I will describe the various utility programs that are available to UUCP administrators, and also give some hints on solving common UUCP problems.

Before I proceed to the individual programs, I'd like to mention the *debug level* option that is available with many of them. The *debug level* is a number from zero to nine. When it is not set to zero, the programs generate, either to the screen or to an output file, a running commentary on what they are doing. The higher the number, the more detail is produced. The resulting data are of varying degrees of usefulness. Sometimes they can be quite helpful in identifying where a program is going wrong. At other times they consist of a series of statements that are incomprehensible unless you are a C programmer and have access to the source code for the utility program concerned.

THE uucheck PROGRAM

The *uucheck* program is used to find certain errors in the UUCP files. If you type

```
/usr/lib/uucp/uucheck
```

uucheck looks to make sure that some of the required files are present, and checks for some inconsistencies in the Permissions file. It will not report on all errors, but it can be useful to run *uucheck* after installing UUCP for the first time.

If you type

```
/usr/lib/uucp/uucheck -v
```

then *uucheck* will perform the above tests, and also give you a report on each remote system, indicating whether it can request files, what local programs it can run, and what local directories it can access.

With either of the above options, you can add the

   -x*debug level*

parameter; see my comments at the beginning of this chapter with regard to this.

THE uutry PROGRAM

The *uutry* program is used for testing the connection to a particular site. The program runs *uucico* with the name of the site, redirecting debugging output to the file /tmp/*sitename*, where *sitename* is the name of the remote site. It is a good idea to run *uutry* after you enter the configuration details for a new site in your system.

The format for the uutry command is as follows:

   uutry [-x *debug level*] [-r] *system name*

The optional -x parameter enables you to change the debug level. The default debug level is 5.

After each unsuccessful attempt to connect to a particular site, UUCP increases the delay before the next time it will allow an attempt to connect to that site. The -r option enables you to order *uutry* to ignore any retry time that has been set for the site by UUCP.

The *uuinstall* program that is provided with SCO UNIX and SCO XENIX includes an option to attempt to connect to a system. Unfortunately, it does not use any equivalent to the -r option, so that working on a connection to a particular site by repeatedly modifying the script file and then attempting to connect can be very frustrating using *uuinstall*.

THE uuclean PROGRAM

At a busy site, UUCP can generate excessive amounts of data, using up valuable space on your disk. The *uuclean* program helps with this problem by getting rid of old files. It also cancels transfers that have not been successfully completed within a specified number of days, and will send *mail* messages to those users whose transfers have been cancelled. It also warns users whose transfers are not being cancelled yet, but have experienced delays.

The options to the uuclean command are as shown in Table 17.1.

As we saw in the last chapter, the script file *uudemon.clean*, often run once a day through *cron*, runs *uuclean* after archiving some of the data that uuclean deletes.

Table 17.1: uuclean options

OPTION	DEFAULT	MEANING
-C*time*	7	Remove any C. (Command) files older than *time* days old
-D*time*	7	Remove any D. (Data) files older than *time* days old
-W*time*	1	Warn the originator about any C. (Command) files older than time *days old*
-X*time*	2	Delete any X. (Execute) files older than *time* days old
-o*time*	2	Delete any other files older than time days old
-xsite	all	Execute only for the named site
-x*debug level*	0	Run at the specified debug level
-m*string*		Include the message *string* in any warning messages

THE uusched PROGRAM

I described in the last chapter how *uudemon.hour* is run at regular intervals through *cron*, and how *uudemon.hour* runs *uusched*. The *uusched* program looks through the spool files for each remote site to see whether there is work for that site, and if there is it runs *uucico* for that site. You will not normally run *uusched* directly.

There are two options for the *uusched* program. The first, -x*debug level*, sets a debug level for uusched. The second, -u*debug level*, sets a debug level to pass through to *uucico*, governing the level of debug messages generated by *uucico*.

THE uulog PROGRAM

UUCP maintains log files of its activities. These files are held in subdirectories under the directory /usr/spool/uucp/.Log. The subdirectories are

/usr/spool/uucp/.Log/uucp

/usr/spool/uucp/.Log/uuico

/usr/spool/uucp/.Log/uux

/usr/spool/uucp/.Log/uuxqt

As you may have guessed, the subdirectories maintain logs of activities performed by the programs after which they are named. In the subdirectories there is one file for each remote system. For example, the log file for *uux* activities related to the remote system *sco* would be /usr/spool/uucp/.Log/uux/sco.

You can examine these log files using any of the UNIX utilities that allow you to look at ASCII files (*vi*, *cat*, and others). However, the uulog command is an easier way. For example, if you are not sure whether a particular connection to a site *sco* was successful you can enter

    uulog -ssco

This command will cause the entries in the log file maintained by *uucico* for sco to be displayed. If you want to look at only the most recent entries, you can use the -f option. The following example would list the ten most recent entries:

    uulog -fsco -10

You can also use uulog to look at the log files maintained by *uuxqt* by using the -x option. You will recall that *uuxqt* is the program that executes commands requested by remote systems. To look at the last five entries made by *uuxqt* for sco, you can enter

    uulog -fsco -x -5

THE uustat PROGRAM

In Chapter 10 I described how users can find the current status of their UUCP file transfers by using the uustat command. uustat also has several options that are mainly of use for administrators. A complete list of uustat options follows.

THE -a OPTION

If you enter

    uustat -a

uustat will list all jobs waiting to be performed. These will typically be messages to be sent to sites that call us but have not called us yet, or to sites that we call at specified times.

THE -m OPTION

You can find out whether the last attempt to connect with each machine was successful by entering

    uustat -m

uustat will list each site, with the date, time, and result of the most recent connection attempt.

THE -p OPTION

The -p option reports on connections that are currently in process at the time you type

    uustat -p

I explained in the last chapter that when UUCP is using a particular device, it creates a file known as a lock file. The -p option instructs *uustat* to examine all lock files, to see which UNIX processes created them, and to list those processes using the UNIX ps command. This is mainly of use in tracking down communications sessions that appear to be stuck.

THE -q OPTION

If you enter

    uustat -q

uustat will report on each site, giving the number of outstanding jobs of each type and the status of that site. For example, you might see a report as follows:

    thatsite 2C   07/30-17:53 WRONG TIME TO CALL

This means that there are two command files for the site *thatsite*. The .Status file, created on July 30 at 5:53 p.m., indicates that a user requested a transfer, but the transfer has not yet taken place because *thatsite* can only be called at certain times.

THE -k OPTION

You can cancel a pending job by using the -k (kill) option. In order to use this option, you need to know the *job-ID* of the job. The job-ID is the first field printed for a job when you list all current jobs using the uustat command. For example, imagine that a user named *dorothy* has sent mail to *oz!wizard*. The message has not yet been transmitted. You could identify the job by typing

    uustat -soz

This will list all current jobs for the site *oz*. The list could include the following entry:

    ozN034a   07/30-18:07   S   oz   dorothy 132 D,sli789834a
               07/30-18:07   S   oz   dorothy rmail wizard

You could cancel this message by typing

    uustat -kozN034a

However, you cannot cancel a job unless you are a superuser, or the user who created the job.

THE -r OPTION

You will remember that *uuclean* deletes files that are older than a specified number of days. Sometimes you may not want a particular message to be deleted. For example, you may know that the site *oz* has been experiencing telecommunications problems and that Dorothy's message has been delayed, but that it should go through in the next two days. The -r option to the uustat command enables you to *refresh* a job by updating its date and time to the current date and time so that *uuclean* will not delete it as an old file. You use the -r option with the job-ID as you would with the -k option. The following command would refresh Dorothy's message, but not once it has been cancelled.

    uustat -rozN034a

THE -s AND -u OPTIONS

The final two options are -s, requesting a list of jobs for a particular site, and -u, requesting a list of jobs originated by a particular user. These can be used in combination. For example,

    uustat -soz -udorothy

requests a list of all current jobs for the site *oz* originated by the user *dorothy*.

THE uucico PROGRAM

I explained in the last chapter how the program *uucico* is the program that actually connects two UUCP systems. The program runs at both ends of the connection: *uucico* on the calling system logs into the remote system, which then runs its own copy of *uucico* to interface with the copy running on the calling system. *uucico* is normally run indirectly: either by *uucp* or by *uusched* on a regular basis. However, you can run *uucico* yourself if you want to make an immediate connection to a particular site to perform any outstanding transfers. The parameters to the uucico command are as follows:

THE ROLE NUMBER

Since *uucico* can either initiate a connection or respond to a remote initiation, you must tell it which role to adopt. A *1* indicates *master mode*, meaning that it is the calling system, and a *0* indicates *slave mode*, meaning that it is the answering system. If you run *uucico* directly in order to connect to a remote system, you will always run it in master mode as follows:

uucico -r1 *sitename*

THE SITE TO CALL

You can specify the site that you want to call in two ways: with -s or with -S. If you use the lowercase version, *uucico* will only call if the current time is appropriate as specified for the site that you are calling. If you use the uppercase version, *uucico* will ignore the setting for time to call, and will call immediately— even if the time to call was specified as "never". The following command forces an immediate call to the site *sco*:

uucico -r1 -Ssco

THE spool DIRECTORY

The normal spool directory for UUCP is /usr/spool/uucp. You can override this directory by using the parameter -d with another directory path.

TROUBLESHOOTING UUCP

UUCP is a complex system, and is used at far more sites and far more frequently than was initially intended. Things do not always run smoothly, and many different problems arise from time to time; the number of UUCP utilities dedicated to troubleshooting and debugging may give you an idea of what to expect. Nevertheless, UUCP has proved to be an invaluable tool in the UNIX community, and until something better shows up we will have to deal with its problems from time to time. In the following sections I will assume that messages you are trying to send to a remote site are not arriving, and suggest some steps you might take to find where the problem is. I will also assume for simplicity that you are not dealing with messages being forwarded via an intermediary site.

LOCATING
THE GENERAL AREA OF THE PROBLEM

The first step is to find out whether the problem is

- a hardware problem,

- a configuration problem at your end, or

- a problem at the remote end.

The following list provides some initial general rules:

1. If all your UUCP transmissions are failing, rather than those for a particular site, suspect a hardware problem or errors in your device configuration files.

2. If UUCP thinks that it has successfully sent the message (i.e., the entry is no longer shown as pending by the uustat command), suspect that the problem is at the remote site.

3. Always check the status file for the site in /usr/spool/uucp/.Status. There should be an error message which should be of some help, although the messages are not always very specific and can actually be misleading. I will deal with some of the individual error messages below.

HARDWARE PROBLEMS

You can take the following steps to troubleshoot hardware problems:

1. Make sure the modem is turned on and receiving power.

2. Make sure the telephone line to the modem is live, by attaching a telephone and listening for a dial tone.

3. Turn the modem off and on again to reset it to the default settings.

4. Use *cu* to talk directly to the modem. See whether it responds. A Hayes modem will respond "OK" or "0 " when you type ATT followed by a carriage return.

5. If the modem does not respond, look at the lights to see whether they flash when you transmit to it. If the lights do not flash, try replacing the cable.

6. If the cable is not defective, try using an alternative modem. If you do not have one available, try using a loop-back connector in place of the modem. This is a connector where the transmit line (pin 2) is connected to the receive line (pin 3). Anything you type using *cu* should be echoed back to your screen.

7. If replacing the modem and cable does not work, suspect the serial interface card. Try using a different port. If you still cannot communicate, the problem may be in the software configuration rather than the hardware.

DECODING UUCP ERROR MESSAGES

The following are some error messages that you can find in the .Status file for the remote site, with some suggestions as to how they arose.

CALLER SCRIPT FAILED   This message means that the interaction with the modem or dialer unit did not proceed as expected. This may mean that the modem is turned off, or that there is a hardware problem. See the steps above concerning hardware problems.

RETRY TIME NOT REACHED   If UUCP fails to make a connection with a remote site, it waits before trying again. With each successive failure the waiting period increases. An easy way to override this waiting period is to delete the file for the remote site in .Status.

LOGIN FAILED   This message can be deceptive. It suggests that you have set up the wrong login or password for the remote site, but it can also mean that the remote site did not answer the telephone. Using the uutry command can help narrow down the problem.

HANDSHAKE FAILED   This message indicates that there is an error in the Permissions file.

DEVICE LOCKED   This message indicates that a lock file exists for the device in /usr/spool/uucp. This probably means that another process is using the same device, in which case all you need to do is try again later. The uustat -p command can indicate which process locked a particular device. Sometimes a lock file will remain for a device even though the device is no longer in use; this is generally caused by a system crash or software error. In this case you can simply delete the lock file.

NO DEVICES AVAILABLE   This message generally indicates that all devices that are capable of connecting with the remote site in question are already in use. You simply need to try later. However, it may also mean that there are inconsistencies in your files: perhaps you entered a device type that does not exist for that site, or a baud rate that is not supported by any device.

PART FOUR

UNIX Communications for Programmers

In the first three parts of this book, I have covered serial communications in general, and UNIX communications at the user and the system administrator level. In Part IV, I will describe UNIX communications for programmers. Chapter 18 will describe how programmers can access serial devices through standard UNIX system calls. In Chapter 19, I will cover various related programming tips and techniques.

18

System Calls
to Access
Serial Devices

In this chapter I will describe the system calls that programmers may use to control serial device drivers. The calls I will describe are based on SCO XENIX. Where I am aware of differences from other versions of UNIX, I will point them out.

THE I/O SYSTEM CALLS

The programming interface to the serial device drivers is through the following seven UNIX system calls:

open()
: Opens a communications session with the device whose name is passed to open(), and returns a file descriptor handle (an integer number) through which future communications with that device will be managed

read()
: Returns one or more characters that have been received by the device, up to the number requested in the read() call

write()
: Requests the device to transmit one or more characters

close()
: Terminates the communications session with the device driver

ioctl()
: Sets a large number of optional communications parameters. Similar in function to the stty command described in Part 3 of this book

fcntl()
: Used to specify whether a read() call will return immediately or wait for the specified number of characters to be received

select()
: Used where more than one device may have data available, and polling is not desirable. Not available on all versions of UNIX

Most of these calls will no doubt be familiar to you, since they are also used for reading and writing disk files. However, the descriptions of the calls here will relate strictly to their use in connection with serial device drivers. In the remainder of this chapter I will describe the system calls in turn.

THE open() CALL

The open() function call is used to gain access to a device driver. The format of the call is

```
int open(path, flags)
char *path;
int flags;
```

RETURNED VALUE

If the open() call is successful, it returns a *file descriptor*, also called the *handle*, a positive integer. You will use the file descriptor in subsequent calls such as read() and write(). If the call is unsuccessful, it returns the value –1, and sets the global variable *errno* to a value that indicates the reason why the call failed. The various values for *errno* are defined in /usr/include/sys/errno.h.

Possible *errno* codes set by open() errors are

ENOENT	The file does not exist
ENXIO	The driver exists, but its physical device is not present
EACCES	The user does not have read and/or write permission (depending on how the file was opened) for this file
EMFILE	Too many files are open
EINTR	A signal occurred and interrupted the open
EBUSY	Another process has gained exclusive use of the device (not supported by all versions of UNIX)

THE PATH PARAMETER

path is the full pathname of the device file that you wish to access, such as

/dev/tty1a

Note that just as with regular files, device files have both individual and group permissions. If the permissions set for the file, and its directory and parent directories, do not allow the user of your program to read and write, the open() command will fail, and *errno* will be set to the value defined as EACCES.

THE FLAGS PARAMETER

The *flags* parameter is an integer, each bit of which represents a different flag. To set a combination of flags, you use the OR instruction (indicated by a vertical line). Most of the flags defined for the open() command relate to disk files. The flags relevant to device files are

O_RDONLY	Open for reading only
O_WRONLY	Open for writing only
O_RDWR	Open for reading and writing (the normal setting)
O_NDELAY	Reads should return immediately instead of waiting for data

A typical setting for the *flags* parameter would be

O_RDWR

PROGRAM EXAMPLE

The code fragment in Figure 18.1 shows how you would normally use the open() system command in conjunction with a special device file.

```
#include <fcntl.h>
#include <errno.h>
main()
{
int f;
        f = open("/dev/ttyla", O_RDWR);
        if (f > 0) {
            printf("Device opened correctly");
        }
        else {
            switch(errno) {
                case (ENOENT):
                    printf("Device driver not found\n");
                    break;
                case (EACCES):
                    printf("You do not have permission\n");
                    break;   . . . . . . . . . . . .
            }
        }
        .
        .
        .
        close (f);
}
```

Figure 18.1: open() with a serial device driver

STANDARD INPUT AND OUTPUT

You do not need to explicitly *open* the standard input and standard output devices, since they are already open when your program is invoked. You can obtain a handle by using the *fileno* macro, as in the following example:

```
#include <stdio.h>

main()

{

int f;

    f = fileno(stdin);

}
```

You can then use the handle in future read(), write(), ioctl(), and fcntl() calls. You will not, of course, close the standard input device.

Note that if input to your program has been redirected, fileno(stdin) will not refer to the device driver controlling input from the terminal. To be sure that you are controlling this device driver, open the driver explicitly as follows:

```
f = open("/dev/tty", O_RDWR);
```

/dev/tty here is a pseudo device for whichever device is really controlling the current process.

THE read() CALL

Once you have opened a device and obtained a handle to it, you can read characters received from the device by using the read() system call.

FORMAT OF THE read() CALL

The format of the call is as follows:

```
int count;

count = read(f, ptr, nbr);
```

where *f* is the file handle returned by the open() call, *ptr* is a pointer to a buffer where you want the characters read to be placed, and *nbr* is the maximum number of characters to read.

Suppose that you have opened a device driver associated with a serial port, and you want to read some characters from it. You will not know at this stage how many, if any, characters have been received. However, you will know how many characters you have room for in your buffer. You specify the maximum number of characters to read in the *nbr* parameter, and the system call returns the actual number of characters that were read.

If a device is in *canonical mode*, read() only returns complete lines up to a new-line character. Canonical mode is described later in this chapter under the discussion of the ioctl() function call.

HOW read() WORKS

Note that read() does not actually instruct the driver to read characters from the serial port. The driver automatically reads characters once it has been opened, as they are received, and stores them in an internal buffer. This process takes place concurrently with whatever else is going on in the system. The read() command asks the driver to copy up to *nbr* characters from its buffer into the buffer pointed to by *ptr*. The driver will then throw away those characters so that the next read() command will return the next characters received.

BLOCKING AND NON-BLOCKING I/O

As we will see later in this chapter, you can use the fcntl() system call to specify *blocking* or *non-blocking* input for a device. This setting affects how read() works in circumstances where no characters are available from the device at the time when you issue the read() call. Although the actual setting is made through fcntl(), I will describe its effects here, since they are relevant to the read() system call.

Blocking

If you specify blocking, read() will return only when one of the following conditions occurs:

- If the device is in canonical mode, a new-line character is received
- At least *VMIN* number of characters have been received
- *VTIME* tenths of a second expire

It is important to remember that read() does not wait for the number of characters that you specified in the third parameter to the read() call—this is the *maximum* number of characters to return. read() will return whichever is the lesser of the number you specified and the number actually available in the input buffer at the time it returns.

VMIN is normally 1, but you can change its value by using the stty() command described later in this chapter.

The read() call will also return after a specified delay. The delay is set by specifying VTIME, in tenths of a second, using ioctl(). If VMIN is zero, the timer starts when the read() call commences: if no characters are received by the time VTIME expires, the driver returns with a count of zero. If VMIN is greater than zero, the timer does not start to run until the first character has been received, and is restarted as each subsequent character is received. Setting VTIME to zero will cause the timer to be ignored.

A signal will also cause a blocked read() to return with a count of zero. I will describe the effect of this in the next chapter.

Non-Blocking

If you specify non-blocking, and no characters are available, the driver will return immediately with a count of zero. If characters are available, the driver will copy whichever is lesser of the number of characters available and the number of characters requested. If canonical mode is set, characters are not considered to be available until a new line has been received. read() will return with a count of zero if only part of a line has been received.

If you are considering using non-blocking i/o, please refer to the next chapter ("Programming Tips and Techniques"), where I discuss the disadvantages from a system efficiency point of view.

THE write() CALL

In order to transmit characters, you use the write() system call. The format of this call is

```
int count;

count = write(f, ptr, nbr)
```

where *f* is the file handle for the device returned by the open() call, *ptr* is a pointer to a buffer containing the characters to transmit, and *nbr* is the number of characters to send.

The call will return the number of characters successfully transferred to the driver's transmit buffer. Note that this does not mean that the characters have actually been transmitted, just that they have been accepted for transmission. For example, if you are using the XON/XOFF protocol and the driver has received an XOFF signal from the remote device, indicating that it does not want any more characters for the time being, then write() will return with a count equal to the number of characters that you sent it, provided that there was room in the buffer, even though the characters have not yet been transmitted. If XON is never received the characters will never be sent. If you want to be sure that data have been received by a remote device, you should implement some type of block transfer protocol.

THE close() CALL

When you have finished with the device, you should issue the close() system call. The format is simply

close(f)

where f is the file handle returned by the original open() call.

THE ioctl() CALL

You will recall from Chapter 14 ("Configuring Ports with *stty*") that there are many ways in which you can configure a device driver by using the stty command. For example, you can specify the baud rate and other communications parameters, and also instruct the driver to add or discard line feeds, respect or ignore interrupt characters, and so on.

The programmer's equivalent of stty is ioctl(). Like stty, ioctl() sets parameters known as *flags*.

FORMAT OF THE ioctl() FUNCTION CALL

The format of the ioctl() function call is

result = ioctl(*f, request, arg*)

where *f* is the file handle returned by the **open**() call, *request* is an integer indicating the instruction given to the driver (for example, to set certain values or to return the current values), and *arg* is a pointer to a structure of the type *termio* described below. ioctl() can be used to control device drivers of various types. The discussion here will be limited to the control of serial devices.

RETURNED VALUE

The result returned by ioctl() will be zero if the call was successful, and −1 if it failed. If the call failed, the global variable *errno* will be set to a corresponding value. Possible values are

EBADF	*f* was not a valid file handle
ENOTTY	*f* was a file handle, but not for a serial device driver
EINVAL	*request* was invalid
EFAULT	Invalid address
EINTR	A signal occurred during the call

REQUEST TYPES

The *request* parameter will be one of the following values:

TCGETA	Read the currently set parameters into the termio structure pointed to by *arg*
TCSETA	Set the parameters according to the settings contained in the termio structure pointed to by *arg*

TCSETAW Wait for output to drain, and then set the parameters according to the settings contained in the termio structure pointed to by *arg*

TCSETAF Wait for output to drain, then flush the input queue and then set the parameters according to the settings contained in the termio structure pointed to by *arg*

THE termio STRUCTURE

Parameters passed to and from ioctl() are contained in a structure of the type *termio*. This structure, and a large number of defined values to assist in using it, are defined in the file /usr/include/sys/termio.h. I suggest that you print out termio.h and look at it while reading this section. The structure definition is as follows:

```
#define NCC 8
struct termio {
    unsigned short c_iflag;
    unsigned short c_oflag;
    unsigned short c_cflag;
    unsigned short c_lflag;
    char c_line;
    unsigned char c_cc[NCC];
}
```

You will see that four of the fields consist of numbers. The individual bits in these numbers represent different parameters, so very many parameters can be saved in only four numbers. I will describe the individual fields, and then give some examples of how to use them.

The c_iflag Field

The c_iflag field contains a set of parameters that are referred to as *input modes.* These parameters enable you to specify

- the type of hardware and software handshaking to use

- how to handle breaks, carriage returns, new-line characters and parity errors

- whether to strip the high bit of each character received

The parameters are as follows:

IGNBRK	Ignore break signals received
BRKINT	Signal an interrupt when a break signal is received
IGNPAR	Ignore parity errors
PARMRK	Mark parity errors
INPCK	Enable input parity check
ISTRIP	Strip the high bit of each character
INLCR	Convert received new-line characters to carriage returns
IGNCR	Ignore received carriage-return characters
ICRNL	Convert received carriage-return characters to new-line characters
IXON	Suspend transmissions when an XOFF character is received; resume when an XON character is received
IXANY	Resume transmissions when any character is received
IXOFF	Send an XOFF character to signal a remote device to suspend transmissions; transmit an XON character to signal it to resume

CTSFLOW   Suspend transmissions when the CTS hardware
            handshaking line from the remote device is low;
            resume transmissions when it is high

RTSFLOW   Lower the RTS (RQS) hardware handshaking line to
            the remote device to signal it to suspend
            transmissions; raise it to signal the device to resume

The c_oflag Field

The next field in the termio structure is the field c_oflag. Like c_iflag, it consists of multiple flags, all defined in termio.h. The flags relate to *post-processing of output*. This means that if any of the flags are set, then the device driver will manipulate in some way the characters that are sent to it before transmitting them out of the serial port.

Most of these flags are rarely used. They relate to antique computer equipment such as printers that can only print in upper case, and equipment that has no input buffer and that actually needs the host computer to wait while it performs some actions such as physically returning the carriage to the left-hand margin. You may need to adjust the flags relating to carriage-return and new-line mapping for some equipment, since some printers automatically generate a line feed when they receive a carriage return and some require both characters. If you find that either a printer is generating an extra blank line after each line, or it is printing all the lines on top of each other, then you probably have this type of mismatch.

The first flag in c_oflag is bit zero, defined as OPOST (post process output). If this bit is clear, the remaining bits will be ignored.

The second flag, OLCUC, instructs the driver to convert transmitted characters to upper case.

The next set of flags defines mapping of new-line and carriage-return characters as follows:

ONLCR   Translate new-line characters to carriage returns

OCRNL   Translate carriage returns to new-line characters

ONOCR   Do not transmit carriage return if column is zero

ONLRET   Assume new-line character triggers carriage return

The final set of flags in c_oflag relates to delays required by the old equipment I mentioned above. Unlike the flags in c_iflag, some of them are defined as combinations of bits rather than individual bits. They are as follows:

OFILL	Transmit fill characters to generate delays
OFDEL	Use the DEL character as the fill character (the default is to use the NUL character)
NLDY	Select new-line delays.
CRDLY	Select carriage-return delays
TABDLY	Select tab-character delays
BSDLY	Select backspace delays
VTDLY	Select vertical-tab delays
FFDLY	Select form-feed delays

In addition to the above flags, there are other settings that indicate how long the delays should be. If you need to use these, you will find them in termio.h.

The c_cflag Field

The c_cflag field contains the information needed to set communications parameters such as baud rate and parity. Common baud rates through 9600 are represented by *B* followed by the baud rate. The defined number CBAUD comprises all the bits that are used to represent the baud rate OR'ed together (see Chapter 19). For example, to set 2400 baud your program could read as follows:

```
#include <termio.h>

set2400(f)

int f;   /* The file handle returned by open() */
```

```
{
struct termio t;
    ioctl(f, TCGETA, &t); /* Read the current settings */
    t.c_cflag &= ~CBAUD;   /* Turn off all baud rate bits */
    t.c_cflag |= B2400;    /* Set bits to represent 2400 */
    ioctl(f, TCSETA, &t); /* Write back the settings    */
}
```

Setting the baud rate to zero (defined as *B0)* will instruct the device driver to lower the DTR signal. You can use this to instruct a modem to hang up, provided that the modem is configured to hang up when DTR is lowered.

There are often two extra baud rate values defined: EXTA and EXTB. These originally referred to serial devices driven by an external clock, but many implementations of UNIX now use these values to specify higher baud rates such as 19,200.

The next pair of bits within c_flag defines the character size. You can specify CS5, CS6, CS7 or CS8 to specify five through eight bits respectively. The defined value CSIZE can be used to turn off any currently set values The following example sets eight data bits:

```
#include <termio.h>
set8bit(f)
int f;   /* The file handle returned by open() */
{
struct termio t;
    ioctl(f, TCGETA, &t); /* Read the current settings */
    t.c_flag &= ~CSIZE;   /* Turn off word length bits */
    t.c_flag |= CS8;      /* Set 8 bits */
    ioctl(f, TCSETA, &t); /* Write back the settings    */
}
```

The remaining flags in c_cflag are more straightforward, since each bit represents only one setting, as follows:

CSTOPB	Set 2 stop bits (if clear, set 1)
CREAD	Enable reads from the device
PARENB	Enable parity
PARODD	Set odd parity (even parity if clear)
HUPCL	Hang up the line when the last process is closed
CLOCAL	The line is connected directly; it is not a dial-up connection
LOBLK	Block the output of a job-control layer if it is not the current layer

The CLOCAL setting affects hardware handshaking signals. If it is not set, a modem is assumed, and the device will not transmit unless the carrier detect signal is present. This makes it hard to write to a modern auto-dial modem that does not assert CD until it is actually on-line!

The c_lflag Field

The last of the flags fields in the termio structure is the c_lflag field. The bits within this field are as follows:

ISIG	Enable signals
ICANON	Enable processing of the erase and kill characters
XCASE	Enable canonical presentation of upper/lower case
ECHO	Echo characters received (full duplex)
ECHOE	Echo the erase character as backspace-space-backspace
ECHOK	Echo a new-line character after receiving the kill character

ECHONL   Echo the new-line character when received, even if
           ECHO is not set

NOFLSH   Disable flushing the buffer when an interrupt or quit
           signal is received

XCLUDE   Gain exclusive use of the line

As you will see, these settings are designed for use when the device connected to the serial line is a terminal.

The ISIG setting tells the device driver to react appropriately when it receives the INTR (interrupt), SWTCH (switch), or QUIT (terminate) character. If the device connected to the serial line is not a terminal, you will probably clear the ISIG flag. Otherwise the receipt of a binary signal could happen to coincide with one of the special characters and cause the device driver to generate an inappropriate signal with unplanned consequences.

The ICANON flag enables *canonical input.* This means that data received are interpreted line by line rather than character by character. Characters received will be retained in the buffer of the device driver until a new-line character is received. Meanwhile, the erase and kill characters will be acted upon and will serve to delete one character or the whole line currently in the buffer, and any read() command to the driver will return a count of zero, unless blocking is set. As with the ISIG flag, the ICANON flag is primarily used in conjunction with terminals. If you are communicating with another type of device you will probably want to process input as it is received, rather than on a line-by-line basis. In that case you should clear the ICANON flag. The result of the read() system call will then depend on the VMIN and VTIME flags described below, and the O_NDELAY flag described later under the fcntl() system call.

The XCLUDE flag is available under SCO XENIX, but not under many other versions of UNIX. It is used to prevent multiple processes from trying to access the same device at the same time. If a process opens a device and sets the XCLUDE flag, the next process will find that the open() call fails and *errno* is set to EBUSY, unless the second process is run under super-user privileges.

The c_line Field

The c_line field is used internally by UNIX to indicate the type of line discipline. You should not change this setting unless you know which line discipline to select. The choices are specific to particular UNIX implementations.

The c_cc Field

The c_cc field is an array of special characters. The following symbolic constants define the offsets into the array for the corresponding characters:

OFFSET	CHARACTER
VINTR	The interrupt key
VQUIT	The quit key
VERASE	The erase key
VEOF	The end-of-file character
VEOL	The end-of-line character
VSWTCH	The switch character

For example, the following program changes the interrupt key to CTRL-C on the device currently being used for standard input:

```
int_ctc()
{
struct termio t;
int f;
    f = fileno(stdin);
    ioctl(f, TCGETA, &t);
    t.c_cc[VINTR] = 3;
    ioctl(f, TCSETA, &t);
}
```

This is a simplified example. In a real program, you would normally save the existing values before changing them, and restore the original values before terminating the program.

If the ISIG flag in c_cflag is clear, the VINTR, VQUIT, and VSWTCH characters will be ignored by the device driver and passed straight through to the calling program. If the ICANON flag in c_cflag is clear, the VERASE, VKILL, VEOF, and VEOL characters will be ignored in the same way. However, the positions in the c_cc array occupied by VEOF and VEOL have a secondary meaning when ICANON is clear: they are also used to specify VMIN and VTIME. These two flags determine the result of the read() system call, and were described earlier in this chapter.

THE fcntl() SYSTEM CALL

The fcntl() system call is used to perform various functions on open files, but when used with serial device drivers it is used to set *blocking* or *non-blocking* mode. You will recall from the description of the read() system call that if blocking mode is set, the read() function will not return until data are present. If blocking is not set, the read() call will return with a count of zero if no data are present. Non-blocking is represented by the flag defined as O_NDELAY. If O_NDELAY is set, then read() will return without delay; otherwise it will wait for data.

The example in Figure 18.2 sets and clears blocking mode. The example starts by reading the current settings. If they are different from the desired settings it then changes them. In the next chapter you will find an explanation of the bit-manipulation techniques used.

THE select() SYSTEM CALL

Imagine that you have opened two or more device drivers, and you want to monitor them for input. You do not know which one will have data first. This can happen in a terminal emulation program, where you do not know whether the next input will come from the keyboard or from the serial port. It can also happen in process control systems, where a

```
#include <fcntl.h>
#include <types.h>

typedef char BOOLEAN;
#define TRUE 1
#define FALSE 0

void set_block(f, mode)
int f;          /* File handle returned bu open() */
BOOLEAN mode;   /* TRUE = block, FALSE = do not block */
{
int flags;
int curmode;

        flags = fcntl(f, F_GETFL, 0);      /* read current settings */
        curmode = !(flags & O_NDELAY);     /* TRUE if blocking set */
        if (curmode != mode) {
                if (mode == TRUE)
                        flags &= ~O_NDELAY;
                else
                        flags |= O_NDELAY;
                fcntl(f, F_SETFL, &flags);
        }
}
```

Figure 18.2: Function to set and clear blocking on a device

program is monitoring input from several different pieces of equipment. One way to handle this situation is to unblock all the devices (set O_NDELAY for each one) and run the program in a loop, reading from each device in turn, and reacting appropriately when read() returns a value greater than zero. However, this method uses a lot of processor time, and can adversely affect performance of the whole system. One alternative is to use the select() system call, although this is not available on all versions of UNIX. Incidentally, at the time of this writing select() does not work under SCO XENIX or SCO UNIX when running on an 80286 machine, or when running on an 80386 machine unless specifically compiled and linked for the 80386.

NOTE

An alternative to using select() is described in the next chapter under "Blocking on Two Devices."

The format of the select() call is as follows:

nfound = select(nfds, readfds, writefds, exceptfds, timeout);

nfds is the file descriptor of the highest numbered device to watch. *readfds, writefds,* and *exceptfds* are pointers to structures of the type *fd_set,* defined in types.h. This structure consists of sufficient long integers to contain one bit for each possible file descriptor; you set the bit corresponding to the file descriptor for each device that you want to watch. *readfds* is the set listing the devices to monitor for data becoming available. *writefds* is the set listing the devices to monitor for becoming available to receive data. *exceptfds* is the set listing the devices to monitor for exception conditions. If you use a null pointer for any of these fd_sets, the corresponding condition will be ignored.

Macros are provided in types.h to simplify the manipulation of the bits in fd_sets as follows:

- **FD_SET(fd, &fdset)** sets the bit corresponding to the file handle *fd* in the fd_set *fdset*

- **FD_CLR(fd, &fdset)** clears the bit corresponding to the file handle *fd* in the fd_set *fdset*

- **FD_ISSET(fd, &fdset)** tests to see whether the bit corresponding to the file handle *fd* in the fd_set *fdset* is set

- **FD_ZERO (&fdset)** sets all the bits in the fd_set *fdset* to zero

The final parameter to **select()** is *timeout.* This is a pointer to a structure of the type *timeval,* defined in select.h. This structure consists of two long integers: *tv_sec,* for the number of seconds, and *tv_usec* for the number of microseconds. If you set *timeout* to zero, or to a null pointer, **select()** will block until data are available from one of the devices; otherwise it will return after the length of time specified in *timeout.*

The return value from **select()**, *nfound,* indicates how many devices met the conditions to be monitored. If an error occurred, *nfound* is − −1. If *nfound* is greater than zero, you can find which device has data available, is ready for writing, or has had an exception occur, by using the FD_ISSET macro for each fd_set and each file number.

Figure 18.3 illustrates using the **select()** call.

In the example, we want to monitor both the communications port and the terminal, and react appropriately to data received from either device. We start by opening the device files controlling each device. We

```
#include <signal.h>
#include <sys/types.h>
#include <fcntl.h>
#include <sys/select.h>

extern int errno;

mainloop()
{
int nfound, hidev;
int tty, asynch;
fd_set readset;

        tty = open("/dev/tty1a", O_RDWR);   /* COM1 */
        if (tty == -1)
                error_exit(errno);    /* An assumed function */

        asynch = open("/dev/tty", O_RDWR); /* The current terminal */
        if (asynch == -1)
                error_exit(errno);            /* An assumed function */

        hidev = max(asynch, tty);

        FD_ZERO(&readset);

        while (doneflag == FALSE) {
                FD_SET(asynch, &readset);
                FD_SET(tty, &readset);
                nfound = select(hidev, &readset, NULL, NULL, NULL);

                if (FD_ISSET(tty, &readset))
                        gettakey();     /* Process a key hit   */

                if (FD_ISSET(asynch, &readset))
                        getcom();       /* Process com input */

        }
}
```

Figure 18.3: Using the select() system call

then initialize an fd_set for reading; we are not concerned with writing or exception events in this example. We compute the highest device number (*nfds*). We then enter a loop; in each pass of the loop we set the flags corresponding to our devices in *readset* using the FD_SET macro, and call select(). We pass a pointer to the fd_set for reading, null pointers for the other sets, and a null pointer for the *timeout* parameter, since we want to block indefinitely until data are received. When select() returns, we check the flags in *readset*, using the FD_ISSET macro, for each device. If the flag representing the communications port is set, we call our communications routine, and if the flag representing the terminal is set we call our keyboard reading routine. Notice that in this example we ignore *nfound*. Since we did not specify a timeout value, select() will not return unless data are available (or, rarely, unless a signal occurred). However, if you specify a timeout period, you could test *nfound* and not call FD_ISSET() unless *nfound* was greater than zero.

19

Programming Tips and Techniques

In the last chapter, I described the system calls that you can use to access and control serial devices. In this chapter, I will describe various programming topics and techniques that are useful in serial communications programming under UNIX.

BIT MANIPULATION IN C

UNIX device drivers often use the individual bits within a byte or an integer to store information. This can be economical—after all, why use an eight-bit byte or a sixteen-bit integer to store a value that can only be 1 or 0?

In this section I will describe the standard techniques for manipulating bits in C.

TERMINOLOGY

Individual bits within a byte or an integer that are used to store boolean values are often referred to as *flags*. A flag is said to be *set* or *turned on* when its corresponding bit has the value of 1, and *clear* or *turned off* when its corresponding bit has the value of 0.

The least significant bit of a number is referred to as *bit zero*. This is the rightmost bit when the number is expressed in binary. The most significant bit of a byte is *bit seven*; the most significant bit of a two-byte integer is *bit fifteen*. These are the leftmost bits when the numbers are expressed in binary.

Each bit within a number can be considered to have what I will refer to as a *bit value*. The bit value of a bit is the value that the number would have if only that bit were set. The bit value of bit zero is 1, since the binary number with only bit zero turned on is 1. The bit value of bit one is 2, and so on as in the following table:

BIT	BIT VALUE
0	1
1	2
2	4
3	8
4	16
5	32
6	64
7	128
8	256
9	512
10	1024
11	2048
12	4096
13	8192
14	16384
15	32768

TESTING A BIT

You may sometimes want to know whether a bit within a number is set. To do this, you logically "AND" the number with its bit value. The logical AND operator in C is the ampersand (&).

The following example tests whether bit four of *myflags* is set

```
if (myflags & 16)

    printf("Bit 4 is set");
```

In the above example, if *myflags* were 40 decimal, C would make the computation shown in Figure 19.1.

```
myflags (40)          0 0 1 0 1 0 0 0
test pattern (16)     0 0 0 1 0 0 0 0
-------------------------------------
AND result            0 0 0 0 0 0 0 0
```

Figure 19.1: Computing 40 AND 16

As you can see, the result is 0, indicating that bit four is not set.

If *myflags* were 52 decimal, C would make the computation shown in Figure 19.2.

```
myflags (52)          0 0 1 1 0 1 0 0
test pattern (16)     0 0 0 1 0 0 0 0
-------------------------------------
AND result            0 0 0 1 0 0 0 0
```

Figure 19.2: Computing 52 AND 16

A non-zero result is produced, showing that bit four is set in *myflags*. You can test for multiple bits at the same time as follows:

```
if (myflags & (16 | 32))

    . . . . .
```

SETTING A BIT

In order to set a particular bit within a number we "OR" the number with the bit value of the bit. Suppose that you want to set bit three. From the above table, you will see that the bit value of bit three is 8. Therefore, to set bit three within a number we OR the number with 8. In C, the symbol for a logical OR is the vertical bar. To set bit three of the variable *myflags* we would enter the following:

```
myflags |= 8;
```

If *myflags* were 37, the computation would be as shown in Figure 19.3.

You can see that the resulting number is the same as the original, except that bit three is now set. The same method works regardless of whether or not bit three was already set.

```
myflags (37)        0 0 1 0 0 1 0 1
test pattern (8)    0 0 0 0 1 0 0 0
-----------------------------------------------
OR result           0 0 1 0 1 1 0 1
```

Figure 19.3: Computing 37 OR 8

We can also set multiple bits at the same time. For example, to set bits eight and nine within a number we could enter

```
myflags |= (256 | 512);
```

CLEARING A BIT

To turn a bit off within a number, we AND the number with the one's complement of the bit value of the bit. In C, the one's complement operator is the tilde (~). This operator sets any bit that is 1 to 0, and any bit that is 0 to 1.

Suppose that you want to turn off bit five within a number. From the table of bit values, you will see that the bit value of bit five is 32. To turn off bit five within a number, you would enter

myflags &= ~32;

If *myflags* were 106 decimal, C would first calculate the byte that is the *one's complement* of 32, as shown in Figure 19.4.

```
          32              0 0 1 0 0 0 0 0
          ˜32             1 1 0 1 1 1 1 1
```

Figure 19.4: 32 and its one 's complement

C would then AND this byte with *myflags* as shown in Figure 19.5.

```
     myflags (106)        0 1 1 0 1 0 1 0
     ˜32                  1 1 0 1 1 1 1 1
     ------------------------------------------------
     AND result           0 1 0 0 1 0 1 0
```

Figure 19.5: Computing 106 AND ~32

You can see that bit five has now been turned off. This works regardless of whether bit five was already cleared.

We can also turn off multiple bits at the same time. To turn off bits three and five, enter

```
myflags &= ~(8 | 32);
```

CODING CONVENTIONS FOR BITWISE OPERATORS

In order to simplify coding, the bit values of various flags within a byte are often defined at the start of a program or in header files. For example, suppose that bit six within a byte indicates that the CTS signal is present, and that bit seven indicates the DSR signal. You could include the following definitions in your program:

```
#define CTS 32    /* bit 6 */
#define DSR 64    /* bit 7 */
```

You could then test *myflags* in the following way to see whether CTS and DSR are both present:

```
if (myflags & (CTS | DSR))
    printf("on line");
else
    printf("disconnected");
```

You will find plenty of examples of these statements in termio.h, and by including that file in your program you can make use of the definitions it supplies.

CIRCULAR BUFFERS

As we saw in Chapter 3, a buffer is an area of memory into which data are placed as a temporary storage space until they can be used. There are three common ways in which this is done.

First, a stack can be used. A stack is an area of memory onto which data are *pushed* and from which they can be *popped.* Data are retrieved from a stack on a *LIFO* (last in first out) basis. This is not very useful for communications programming, since generally speaking you want to retrieve data in the same order in which they arrived (*FIFO,* or first in first out).

Secondly, an area of memory consisting of a sequence of memory locations can be used. Characters are written into sequential locations within this area. When they are needed, they are read back from the start of the memory area. This type of buffer is often used by UNIX internally, where it is referred to as a *clist* or character list. The method is useful when data are being dealt with on a line-by-line basis. It can also be used when data are received one line at a time and retrieved in units of less than a line, provided that there is a handshaking mechanism to prevent a new line from being received until the first one has been retrieved. However, if data are being received and retrieved one character at a time, an alternative method must be found.

The third method is to use a *circular* or *ring* buffer. Like the *clist*, it consists of a sequence of memory locations. However, when the last available location has been used the next character is placed at the beginning of the buffer. Pointers are maintained showing where the next character received is to be placed, and showing the location of the next character to be retrieved. With a circular buffer, if data are received faster than they are being retrieved, the oldest data are overwritten first; however, properly implemented handshaking should prevent characters from being received when the buffer is full. A general method of programming a circular buffer is shown in Figure 19.6 and described below.

CREATING THE BUFFER

First, an area of memory is allocated and the following variables are set up:

r.*size*	The size of the buffer
r.*start*	A pointer which will always point to the oldest character in the buffer
r.*count*	The number of characters currently in the buffer

```
typedef    struct {
    int count;                      /* number of chars now in the buffer    */
    int start;                      /* offset of next characte to take      */
    int size;                       /* size of the buffer                   */
    char *buffer;                   /* Address of the buffer                */
} RING;

/*_____*/
void initbuf(r, addr, len)
register RING *r;
char *addr;
int len;

/*
 * initialize a RING buffer
 */

{
    r -> count   = 0;
    r -> start   = 0;
    r -> buffer  = addr;
    r -> size    = len;
}
/*_____*/
void putbuf(r, ch)
register RING *r;
char   ch;

/*
 * Put a character into a RING buffer
 */

{
int offset;

    offset = (r -> start + r -> count) % r -> size;
                                            /* Position for new char    */

    r -> buffer[offset] = ch;               /* place char in buffer     */

    if (r -> count >= r -> size) {
                                            /* overflow?                */
        r -> start++;                       /* move starting point      */

        if (r -> start >= r -> size)        /* Start is beyond end      */
            r -> start -= r -> size;        /* Rotate it                */

    }

    else {
        r -> count++;                       /* just update the count    */
    }
}
/*_____*/
int getbuf(r, ch)
register RING    *r;
char *ch;
/*
 * Get a character from a RING buffer
 * Returns 0 if buffer is empty.
 */
{
```

Figure 19.6: Circular Buffer functions

```
        if (r -> count == 0)              /* Nothing there       */
            return (0);                   /* return 'failure'    */

        *ch = r -> buffer[r -> start];    /* get next char to take */

        r -> start++;                     /* move starting point */

        if (r -> start >= r -> size) {    /* Do not overflow     */
           r -> start = 0;
        }

        r -> count--;                     /* One less char there */

        return(1);                        /* return 'success'    */
}
/*_____*/
```

Figure 19.6: Circular Buffer functions (continued)

ADDING CHARACTERS

The offset into the buffer for the new character is calculated as follows:

offset = r.start + r.count;

if (offset == r.size) offset −= r.size;

The character is then placed at offset *r.offset* into the buffer. Remember that the first location is offset zero. Thus if the buffer is 128 bytes, the highest offset will be 127, not 128.

After adding the character, we re-compute the pointers. If *r.count* (the number of characters present) is less than *r.size* (the space that is available) we increment *r.count* to allow for the new character. Otherwise, we know that the buffer is full, and we increment *r.start*, cycling it back to the beginning of the buffer if it has reached the end.

RETRIEVING CHARACTERS

If *r.count* is zero, there are no characters available. Otherwise, the character to retrieve is at offset *r.start*. We then increment *r.start* so as to point to the next character, cycling it back to the start of the buffer if it has reached the end.

BLOCKING ON TWO DEVICES BY FORKING

In the previous chapter, I described the **select**() system call, and how you can use it to wait for data from one of a set of devices without incurring the system overhead of constantly polling. However, the **select**() call is not present on all versions of UNIX (and in some versions it is present but does not work!). Fortunately, there is another method available. By using the **fork**() system call, you can cause your program to generate a second instance of itself that runs in parallel, starting at the point where the fork occurred. The procedure is as follows:

1. The program creates a low-level pipe.

2. The program **fork**()s.

3. The main process (the *parent*) issues a blocking **read**() on one device, such as the serial port.

4. The second process (the *child*) issues a blocking **read**() on the other device, such as the keyboard.

5. When a character is received at the serial port, the **read**() issued by the parent returns with a count greater than zero, and the parent deals with the character appropriately and loops back to **read**() the serial port again.

6. When the **read**() issued by the child on the keyboard returns, the child sends a signal to its parent using **signal**() and passes the received data using the pipe. When the signal occurs, the **read**() issued by the parent on the serial port returns with a count of zero and *errno* set to EINTR. The parent wakes up, and sees from the count of zero and the value of *errno* that it was the child that interrupted its sleep, and reads the pipe to obtain the data passed.

This procedure is illustrated in Figures 19.7 and 19.8.

Notice that I have also implemented handshaking between the child and parent. When the child signals the parent to indicate that it has placed data in the pipe, it sets the variable *ack* to FALSE. When the parent receives

```
#include <signal.h>

#define PIPE_READ 0
#define PIPE_WRITE 1

static int kb_pipe[2];
static int child_pid; /* process id of the child process          */
extern int kb;        /* File handle for keyboard                 */
extern int asynch;    /* File handle for coms                     */
int kb_char;          /* Keyboard character                       */
void gotsig();
/*-----------------------------------------------------------------*/
parent()
{
int mypid = getpid();
char comc;

    pipe(kb_pipe);                        /* check return code in real life */
    if ((child = fork()) == 0)            /* If we are in the child:        */
        kbhand(kb_pipe[PIPE_READ], mypid); /* Call the keyboard handler     */

/* notice that the child process never reaches this point */
/* because when we have finished with it we kill it.      */

    (void) signal(SIGUSR1, gotsig);

    for (;;) {
        count = read(asynch, &comc, 1); /* Assuming we have blocked asynch  */
                                        /* read() returns on data or signal */
        if (count > 0)                  /* Got data from coms               */
            com_proc(comc);             /* assumed fn to handle coms input  */
        else {                          /* No data from coms                */
            if (kb_char) {              /* gotsig() read a character        */
                if (kb_char == 27)      /* substitute your own exit key     */
                    break;
                kb_proc(kb_char);       /* assumed fn to handle kb input    */
                kb_char = 0;
            }
        }
    }

    (void) kill(child_id, SIGKILL);
    exit(0);

}
/*-----------------------------------------------------------------*/
void gotsig()
{
/* Called when child signals us to tell us it has got something */

    (void) signal(SIGUSR1, gotsig);
    (void) read(kb_pipe[PIPE_READ], &kb_char, sizeof(kb_char));
    (void) kill(child_id, SIGUSR1); /* Tell child we received message */

}
/*-----------------------------------------------------------------*/
```

Figure 19.7: Blocking on two devices: parent

the signal and deals with the data, it signals the child to indicate that it has received the data. This signal causes the function ackit() to be called which sets the variable *ack* to be TRUE.

```
#include <signal.h>

static int ack;      /* flag used to indicate parent has acknowledged   */
extern int kb;       /* File handle for keyboard                        */
/*-------------------------------------------------------------------------*/
kbhand(pipef, parent)
int pipef, parent;
{
char c;
int count;
void termit();
extern int kb;

/* This is the keyboard handler that runs in the child process */

/* Set up to call ackit() when the parent signals us to say it has */
/* received our signal */

    (void) signal(SIGUSR1, ackit);

    for (;;) {  /* Infinite loop */
        count = read(kb, &c, 1);  /* Get one character. Assume we have already
                                     blocked */
        if (count > 0) {
            ack = 0;
            (void) write(pipef, &c, sizeof(c));  /* Send to the parent   */
            (void) kill(parent, SIGUSR1);        /* Signal parent        */
            while (!ack)                         /* Wait for acknowledge */
                (void) pause();
        }
    }
}
/*-------------------------------------------------------------------------*/
ackit()
{
/* This is called when we get a SIGUSR1 signal from the parent */

    (void) signal(SIGUSR1, ackit);  /* Re-instate the signal trap */
    ack = TRUE;                      /* Set acknowledge flag       */

}
/*-------------------------------------------------------------------------*/
```

Figure 19.8: Blocking on two devices: child

ERROR-CHECKING
CODES COMPUTATIONS

Very often we want to ensure that a block of data being transmitted or stored has not been changed in any way by the time it is received. This is especially important when noise is liable to affect the transmission, such as with the telephone system, or when storage media are subject to damage.

HOW ERROR-CHECKING CODES WORK

A common way to do this is to compute a number, known as an error-checking code, that is mathematically related to the data. This number is transmitted or stored together with the data. When the data are received or retrieved, the number is re-computed and compared with the original number; if the two numbers do not agree, the data must have been changed in some way.

Note that error-checking codes are not one hundred percent effective. It is always possible that the data are changed in such a way that compensating errors occur and the error-checking code remains the same. This is more likely to occur with simple codes such as the *checksum*, which is obtained simply by adding up all the individual bytes in the block. Considerable mathematical research has gone into finding reliable methods for computing an error checking-code; the most common method used now is the *cyclical redundancy check* (CRC). The CRC has two advantages over the checksum. First, it catches a much higher proportion of errors. Second, it is bit-oriented rather than byte-oriented, which means that it can work with protocols that produce a stream of bits rather than a stream of bytes.

THE CYCLICAL REDUNDANCY CHECK

I have yet to see an explanation of CRC calculations that did not appear to assume a degree in advanced mathematics. Since most of my readers are not advanced mathematicians, I will try to explain the calculations in simple terms.

There are several different CRC calculations. In each case, the stream of bits comprising the message is treated as one huge binary number. First, a number (n) of zeros are added to the end of the huge number, to multiply it by 2^n. Then, the number (now even larger) is divided by a number (d) that varies depending on which CRC standard is being used. Only the remainder is retained. This number is transmitted to the receiving device, which then performs the same calculation to make sure the two numbers agree and that no data have been lost or corrupted.

Different communications programs use different versions of CRC. XMODEM, with the CRC option, uses CRC-CCITT. So does Kermit. SDLC uses a modified version of CRC-CCITT. Bisynch uses CRC-16 with EBDIC and CRC-12 with Six Bit Transcode. With ASCII text, Bisynch uses different methods (vertical/longitudinal checks).

Each CRC calculation performs calculations slightly differently. In the case of CRC-16,

n = 16

and

d = 11000000000000101

In the case of CRC-CCITT,

n = 12

and

d = 1100000001111

The number (d) that is divided into the huge number is known as a *generator polynomial*. The polynomial is expressed in the following formula (using CRC-CCITT as an example):

$$X^{16} + X^{12} + X^{5} + 1$$

This expression shows which bits are set in the number used to divide the huge number.

This description explains how CRCs are calculated. However, learning how to program your equipment so that it performs CRC checks is a complicated matter. Specialized communications equipment already incorporates hardware specially designed to do CRC calculations. For more information, read *Technical Aspects of Data Communications* by John E. McNamara (Bedford, Mass.: Digital Press, 1982).

COMPUTING THE CRC IN C

The function in Figure 19.9 calculates the CRC-CCITT and comes from a public-domain program. I am grateful to Chuck Forsberg and Stephen

```
unsigned onecrc(crc, cp)
register unsigned int crc;
char cp;

{
register int count;
unsigned c;

    c = cp & 255;

    for (count = 8; --count >= 0; ) {
        if (crc & 0x8000) {
            crc <<= 1;
            crc += (((c <<= 1) & 0400) != 0);
            crc ^= 0x1021;
        }

        else {
            crc <<= 1;
            crc += (((c <<= 1) & 0400) != 0);
        }
    }

    return(crc);
}
```

Figure 19.9: CRC-CCITT calculation function

Satchell for drawing it to my attention.

The variable *crc* should be initialized to zero, and the function should be called for each character in the string.

A

Common Pin
Connections

Pin	Circuit	Abbreviation	Full name	Direction
Data:				
2	BA	TXD	Transmitted data	DTE to DCE
3	BB	RXD	Received data	DCE to DTE
Primary handshaking lines:				
6	CC	DSR	Data set ready	DCE to DTE
20	CD	DTR	Data terminal ready	DTE to DCE
Secondary handshaking lines:				
4	CA	RQS	Request to send	DTE to DCE
5	CB	CTS	Clear to send	DCE to DTE
Modem lines:				
8	CF	CD	Carrier detect	DCE to DTE
22	CE	RI	Ring indicator	DCE to DTE
Ground or common:				
7	AB	SG	Signal ground	
Less commonly used circuits:				
1	AA		Protective ground	
12	SCF		Secondary received line signal det.	DCE to DTE
13	SCB		Secondary clear to send	DTE to DCE
14	SBA		Secondary Transmitted Data	DTE to DCE
15	DB		Transmitter signal element timing	DCE to DTE
16	SBB		Secondary received data	DCE to DTE
17	DD		Receiver signal element timing	DCE to DTE
19	SCA		Secondary request to send	DTE to DCE
21	CG		Signal quality detector	DCE to DTE
23	CH		Data signal rate selector	DTE to DCE
23	CI		Data signal rate selector	DCE to DTE
24	DA		Transmitter signal element timing	DTE to DCE

Figure A.1: The full set of RS-232 circuits

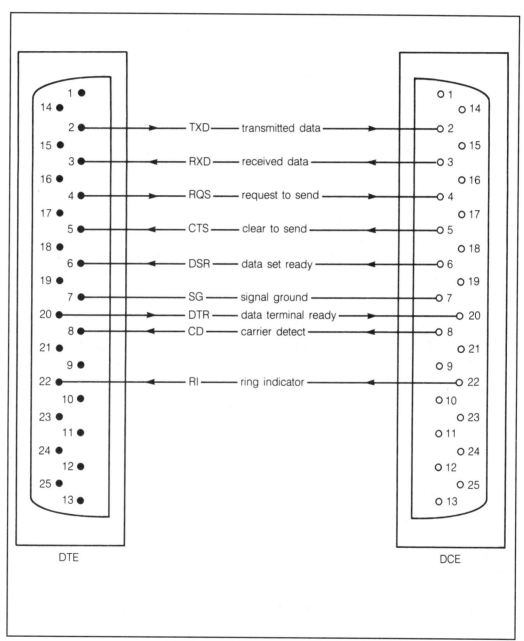

Figure A.2: Standard DTE (e.g., IBM PC) to DCE (e.g., modem) connections

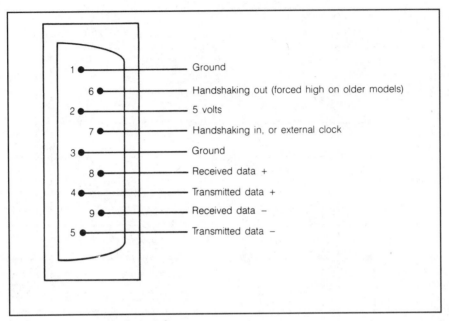

Figure A.3: Macintosh serial port

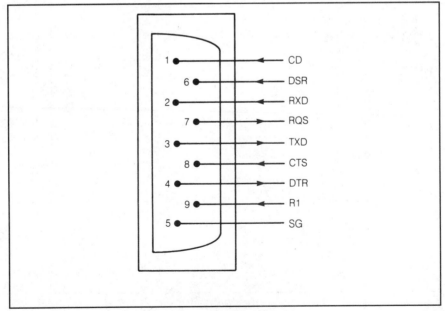

Figure A.4: DB-9 connector used in the IBM PC-AT

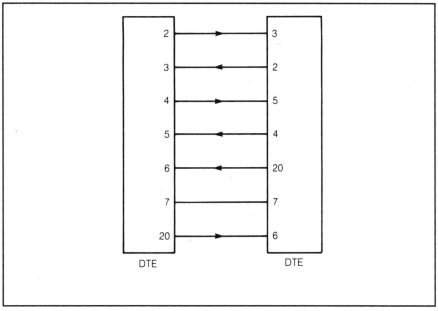

Figure A.5: Null modem connections

B

The XMODEM

Protocol

I am indebted to Ward Christensen, the author of XMODEM, for the following short history, and for clarifying various aspects of the XMODEM protocol.

In September 1977 Ward wrote a program for CP/M-80 that allowed him to exchange programs with other CP/M users. The original program, called MODEM, was intended to be used by two people, one at each computer, at opposite ends of the phone line. When David Jaffe invented BYE, which allows an unattended CP/M computer to be operated by another machine linked by modem, the need arose for an unattended version of MODEM. At this time, many people were revising MODEM itself, and it was taking on new version names such as MODEM7. While Ward's original MODEM program could be used on an unattended machine, the user had to remember to say Q (for Quiet mode). Keith Petersen stripped down MODEM and made XMODEM, which allowed transfer to and from unattended machines.

The protocol implicit in Ward's original program, which some called "the Christensen protocol," has become widely known as the XMODEM protocol.

XMODEM is used most often to download all types of binary and ASCII files from dial-in home computer systems, such as PCs, CP/M machines, etc. However, in spite of its heritage of micro-to-micro communications, XMODEM is also used in mainframe communications where the mainframe is capable of supporting it. CompuServe is a notable example of a mainframe communication system that offers XMODEM file transfers.

BLOCKS

Data transferred by XMODEM are divided up into blocks. Each block consists of a start-of-header character (01 Hex), a one-byte block number, the ones complement of the block number, 128 bytes of data, and a one-byte checksum. This format is illustrated in Table B.1.

Table B.1: XMODEM block format

OFFSET	CONTENTS
0	SOH (start-of-header character: ASCII 01)
1	Block number: starting with 1, but wrapping to 0 after FF
2	Ones complement of the block number (255–block number)
3 to 130	128 bytes of data
131	Checksum: sum of the data bytes only, carry ignored

The block number starts at 1, but is computed modulo 256, meaning that after 255 (FF Hex) it goes back to zero. The one's complement can be computed by subtracting the block number from 255 or by complementing all the bits in the number (turning ones to zeros and zeros to ones). The checksum is a single byte computed by adding together the 128 data bytes and ignoring any carry.

FILE-LEVEL PROTOCOL

Before the sending computer can send data, it has to receive a NAK (negative acknowledgment) character from the receiver. The receiver program is supposed to send a NAK character (15 Hex) as a *timeout* after every ten seconds that go by (officially, but in practice sometimes more frequently) without receiving data. It is the first such NAK that triggers the transmitter to start sending.

Once the receiver program starts receiving a block, it reports an error whenever a gap of one second or more occurs between characters in the block, including the checksum. However, it must wait for the line to clear before sending a NAK to indicate an error.

Note that the one-second timeout is not sufficient for many long-distance connections, and a longer wait is often substituted for the one officially specified.

The receiver then checks the block number and reports an error if it is out of sequence. If the block number is the same as the last one, it indicates a retransmission that should not be considered an error. After receipt of each block, the receiver sends ACK (06 Hex) if the block is received correctly, or NAK if it is not. In the latter case, the transmitter resends the block. After the block is acknowledged, the *next* block is transmitted.

At the end of transmission, the transmitter sends EOT (04 Hex) and waits for an ACK, resending the EOT if it does not get one.

THE CRC OPTION

Because the one-byte checksum is not sufficient to detect all errors, an extension to XMODEM, known as the CRC option, has been devised with a two-byte figure. This figure is called a cyclical redundancy check (CRC-16) and detects errors at least 99.99% of the time. CRCs are explained in Chapter 10.

By convention, the receiver must indicate to the sender that the CRC option is to be used by sending the character C instead of NAK to request the start of transmission. Since not all versions of XMODEM incorporate the CRC option, the receiver should switch to sending NAK if no response is received after several C attempts. The block format using the CRC option is shown in Table B.2.

Table B.2: XMODEM block format with the CRC option

OFFSET	CONTENTS
0	SOH (start-of-header character: ASCII 01)
1	Block number: starting with 1, but wrapping to 0 after FF
2	Ones complement of the block number (255–block number)
3 to 130	128 bytes of data
132	CRC high byte
133	CRC low byte

YMODEM ENHANCEMENTS

YMODEM is XMODEM with some enhancements. The protocol was devised by Chuck Forsberg of Omen Technology, Inc., and is gaining ground. The features that it adds to XMODEM are listed below:

- CRC-16 error checking, as discussed above.

- Optional 1K blocks. Sending STX (02 Hex) at the start of each block instead of SOH (01 Hex) signifies that the block that follows is to be 1024 bytes instead of 128 bytes. Mixed blocks of 1024 bytes and 128 bytes can be sent in a single transmission.

- CAN-CAN abort. Two consecutive CAN (18 Hex) characters indicate that the file transfer is to be aborted.

- Batch-file transmission. Several files can be sent at once. For each file a block numbered zero is sent. This block contains the file name in lower case, terminated by ASCII 0. The file name can include a path name, in which case it is delimited by a forward slash (/), as is the convention in the UNIX system, not a backslash (\) as in MS-DOS systems.

Block zero can also have any of the following four additional fields:

1. The file size as a decimal string followed by a space. If the file size is sent, the receiving program will know which padding characters in the last block, if any, to disregard.

2. The modification date as an octal number measured in seconds from Jan 1 1970 Greenwich Mean Time, with zero if the date is unknown, followed by a space. Using Greenwich Mean Time avoids problems that can arise when people in different time zones are working on a file and it is not clear which is the latest version.

3. A file mode as an octal string (UNIX systems only), followed by a space.

4. A serial number as an octal string. The field is set to zero if there is no number.

The rest of the block is set to nulls. Further files are sent, each with its own file-name block. A null file name terminates batch transmission.

Note that many host computers, and some networks, cannot handle continuous 1K blocks. However, YMODEM supports software handshaking using XON/XOFF, which, depending on the networks and mainframes being used, may allow the transmission of 1K blocks.

XMODEM ADVANTAGES AND DISADVANTAGES

XMODEM's main advantages are its simplicity and its universality. It does have several disadvantages, however, that result primarily from the fact that it is often used in ways it was not originally intended.

It is not capable of solving the word-length problem discussed in Chapter 7. No special transformations take place to allow eight-bit data to be sent with seven-bit communications parameters. Accordingly, if binary data are being sent, eight-bit communications must be possible. The protocol specifies eight data bits, no parity, and one stop bit, even if only seven-bit text data are being transmitted.

Also, there is no protection against binary data being misinterpreted as control signals. If the receiving device, for example, always treats ASCII 4 as meaning the end of transmission, you can only send three blocks, since block four will contain ASCII 4 as its block number. This means that even if the data to be transferred are in acceptable ASCII format the protocol itself can add unacceptable codes.

There is no requirement for full-duplex communications, since the receiving device must wait for transmissions to cease before sending NAK. However, this can result in delays, especially over long-distance links. More sophisticated protocols allow one block to be acknowledged or rejected while a later block is being sent.

While XMODEM has its shortcomings, several of which are addressed in YMODEM, and while more efficient and clever protocols have been and will be implemented, XMODEM retains its popularity because of its universality and ease of implementation.

C

The Kermit
Protocol

The Kermit protocol was developed at Columbia University in New York, primarily to facilitate file transfer between mainframe computers and microcomputers. Kermit is useful for users who want to use a mainframe computer as a storage medium or as an intermediary. With Kermit they can upload programs they have written to the mainframe for subsequent downloading by others, even though the programs are not executable by the mainframe itself.

Kermit has been widely accepted, especially in the academic world, and versions now exist for all major computers. These various versions tend to be circulated from hand to hand. There are both public-domain and copyrighted (but freely distributed) Kermit programs that not only include the protocol but are complete programs in themselves, offering the communications functions needed for the particular machine on which they are running. Accordingly, the name *Kermit* is sometimes used to refer to the protocol and sometimes to a program incorporating it. We will deal only with the protocol here.

Recently, commercial packages have started to offer Kermit as an option. However, Columbia requests that, in keeping with the spirit in which they made the protocol freely available, people incorporating it into commercial products should not charge for doing so. Columbia does maintain a copyright on its own Kermit programs and documentation, so, strictly speaking, Kermit is not in the public domain.

USING KERMIT

The normal method of using Kermit to transfer to and from a mainframe is to start with a communications program running on the microcomputer that incorporates both a terminal emulator and the Kermit protocol. Using the micro as a terminal emulator, the user instructs the mainframe to run its own version of Kermit. Then the microcomputer is switched into Kermit mode and the file transfer can proceed. There are optional server commands that enable the microcomputer to send a number of commands to the mainframe while still in Kermit mode. However, this facility is not always implemented.

SYSTEM REQUIREMENTS

Kermit makes very few demands on the communications capacities of the two machines it is running on. It can cope with systems limited to seven-bit characters, even when the data to be transmitted are in eight-bit form. No handshaking is required other than that provided in Kermit itself. Full-duplex operation is not required for basic operation.

CHARACTER ENCODING

Unlike XMODEM, Kermit does transform all transmitted characters into standard printable characters (ASCII 32 through 126). This way, non-printable characters can be transmitted without causing the receiving computer, or intervening communications equipment, to handle them in special ways.

CONTROL CHARACTERS

Control characters are characters 0 through 31, and 127. When these characters are found in the data to be sent, Kermit translates them into printable characters by "XORing" them with 64 and preceding them by a prefix character (normally #). Thus, Ctrl-A, which is ASCII 1, becomes A, which is ASCII 65, and is transmitted as #A. When the receiving program detects the prefix character, it discards it and converts the following character back to a control character by XORing it with 64. If the prefix character itself is to be sent, it is sent twice—for example, ##.

EIGHT-BIT TO SEVEN-BIT CONVERSION

Kermit can take characters that must consist of eight bits (i.e., extended characters or binary data) and convert them to seven bits. This is necessary when either computer, or the intervening communications path, is not capable of handling eight-bit characters. Kermit checks each character to see whether bit seven is set (i.e., the character is greater than 127). If bit seven is set, the character is preceded by a quoting character (normally &). The character itself is then sent as a seven-bit character. Since this adds considerably to the length of the transmission, it should be avoided whenever eight-bit characters can be sent.

KERMIT INFORMATION CHARACTERS

Characters that do not form part of the data being transmitted but that contain numeric information internal to Kermit, such as the length of a packet, are encoded by adding 32 (unless otherwise stated); this function is known as the *tochar()* function. For example, to indicate a packet length of 26, the number 26 must be sent in the LEN field of the packet. Kermit adds 32 to 26 and sends the ASCII character that corresponds to the total, which in this case is the colon, or ASCII 58.

The corresponding decoding function is the *unchar()* function; it decodes characters known to represent internal Kermit numeric information by subtracting 32 from all characters passed to it.

The greatest number that the tochar() function can encode is 94. This is because 95 plus 32 equals 127, which is a control character, and any characters greater than 127 require eight bits. Accordingly, 94 is something of a magic number within Kermit because it limits the size of various parameters.

Characters that represent themselves (for example when a device wants to indicate to another device which character it wants to precede control characters) are sent as themselves; no special encoding is necessary.

COMPRESSION

When long sequences of the same character are sent, Kermit can compress them. It sends a sequence consisting of a repeat character, which is normally a tilde (~), followed by the repeat count, followed by the character to be repeated. Since the repeat count must be stored in a single character encoded with the tochar() function, the maximum repeat count is 94.

Control characters and eight-bit characters can be repeated; when they have been encoded as two characters (see above) both characters are sent following the repeat count.

PACKETS

The primary message unit used by Kermit is the packet. A packet can consist of data or other information such as acknowledgment or error messages. The types of packets are listed below. Each type is designated by a letter of the alphabet that is stored in the type field of the packet:

D   Data packet

Y   Acknowledge (ACK)

N   Negative acknowledge (NAK)

S   Send initiate (exchange parameters)

B   Break transmission (EOT)

F   File header

Z   End of file (EOF)

E   Error

T   Reserved for internal use

I   Initialize (exchange parameters)

A   File attributes

R   Receive initiate

C   Host command, containing Server commands to the mainframe

K   Kermit command

G   Generic Kermit command

As you can see, Kermit uses these packets to send all sorts of information between communicating computers, from initiation signals to end-of-file information, as well as actual data.

GENERAL PACKET FORMAT

The general packet format is illustrated in Table C.1. The length of individual packets is variable, and packets of different lengths can be sent in one transaction. However, according to the standard protocol, the maximum total packet length is 96 characters. The LEN field, which is the second field in each packet, contains the number of characters following the LEN field up to and including the CHECK field. Thus, LEN would be 94 for the longest permitted packet of 96 bytes. (See the section on long packets later in this chapter for exceptions to this rule.)

Each packet has a sequence number, starting with zero for the initialization packet. The number is modulo 64, meaning that it returns to zero after 63.

Table C.1: Kermit packet format

OFFSET	CONTENTS	MEANING
0	MARK	Normally ^A to mark start of packet
1	LEN	Number of ASCII characters after this field
2	SEQ	Sequence number, modulo 64, starting at 0
3	TYPE	Packet type
4 ...	DATA	Contents of the packet, if applicable
[end]	CHECK	Checksum

INITIATING THE TRANSACTION

A transaction is started when the transmitting device sends an initiation packet containing various parameters. This is acknowledged by the receiving device, which in turn indicates, in the ACK packet, which parameters and options it can support. For example, the sending device may be able to handle eight-bit words but does not know whether the receiving device has this capability. The initiation sequence establishes what common ground exists.

In some cases the exchange of information can take place without automatically being followed by a file transfer. In this case the initialization packets are known as *Init-Info packets* and are type I.

INITIALIZING PACKETS

The packet that the sender transmits to initiate a transaction, and that is normally sent repeatedly until acknowledged, contains six basic characters and a number of additional characters of information in its data field. The acknowledgment packet contains similar information regarding the receiving device. The required fields are listed below:

MAXL   Maximum length of packet that can be received

TIME   Number of seconds the other device should wait before reporting a timeout

NPAD   Number of padding characters that should precede each incoming packet

PADC   Control character required for padding

EOL   Character required to terminate an incoming packet, if any

QTCL   Character used to precede control characters (this is normally #)

The initialization packet can also contain the following optional information:

QBIN   Character used to precede characters that have the eighth bit set when the parity bit cannot be used for data

CHKT   Indicates the check type: 1 means one-character checksum; 2 means two-character checksum; 3 means three-character CRC-CCITT

REPT   Prefix used to indicate a repeated character: space (32) means no repeat count processing; tilde (~) is the normal repeat prefix

CAPAS   A bit mask indicating various KERMIT capabilities. Each bit is set to 1 if the capacity is present. Each character in the field consists of six bits, transformed into a printable character.

QBIN is the character used to precede characters that have the eighth bit set when the parity bit cannot be used for data. It must be different from the QTCL character. A Y response in this field agrees to do eight-bit quoting if requested, N refuses to do eight-bit quoting, and the ampersand (&) or any other character in the ranges of 33– 62 or 96 –126 agrees to do eight-bit quoting with the character used. Normally the ampersand is used if eight-bit quoting is to be done (i.e., the program knows it is dealing with a seven-bit channel).

The CAPAS character(s) contains information about the capabilities being requested (if sent by the transmitting device) or authorized (if sent by the receiving device). There will generally be only one CAPAS byte, but more can be added by setting the low-order bit of the last byte. Table C.2 illustrates the format of the first two CAPAS bytes. The third and subsequent characters are also available for users.

DATA TRANSFER

Once the initialization packets have been exchanged, the data to be sent are transmitted as a series of data packets. The receiving device must respond to each packet with an acknowledgment packet. The transmitting device must wait for each packet to be acknowledged before sending another packet. If the receiving computer reports an error by sending a NAK packet, the sending computer retransmits the packet.

If a NAK packet is received for a packet, this is treated as an equivalent of an acknowledgment of the previous packet. If a packet arrives more than once, the receiver sends an acknowledgment packet and discards the duplicate.

Several files can be sent in one transaction. For each file, Kermit sends a file-header packet, one or more data packets, and an end-of-file packet.

Table C.2: Kermit capability bytes

FIELD #	BIT	MEANING
A: First Character		
1	5	Reserved
2	4	Windowing
3	3	A packets (file attributes)
4	2	Long packets
5	1	Reserved
	0	1 if another CAPAS follows
B: Second Character		
6	5	Reserved
7	4	Reserved
8	3	Available for users
9	2	Available for users
10	1	Available for users
	0	1 if another CAPAS follows

Some implementations of Kermit also send a type-A packet after the file-header packet. This packet contains additional information about a file such as its date of creation, size, and type (e.g., ASCII, EBDIC, or binary). When there are no more files to send, the transmitting computer sends an end-of-transmission packet. The interchange of packets is illustrated in Table C.3.

INTERRUPTING TRANSFER

Kermit has an optional feature that enables file transfer to be interrupted. Sending an EOF packet with a D in the data field means "discard the file." The EOF packet should still be acknowledged. Sending an ACK packet with an X in the data field means "interrupt this file." Sending an

Table C.3: Kermit transaction sequences

EVENT NAME	SENDER TO RECEIVER	RECEIVER TO SENDER
SEND INIT (send initiate)	Parameter packet	
ACK (acknowledge)		Parameter packet
HEADER (file header)	Header packet	
ACK		Acknowledge packet
DATA (data packet)	Data packet	
ACK		Acknowledge packet
[loop to DATA if more data to send]		
EOF (end of file)	EOF Packet	
ACK		Acknowledge packet
[loop to HEADER if more files to send]		
EOT (end of transaction)	EOT packet	
ACK		Acknowledge packet

ACK packet with Z in the data field means "interrupt the whole batch of files."

A fatal error at either end is indicated by an error packet, which terminates the transaction. This should be sent if the above procedures do not work, since it is possible that the other device does not support the interruption options.

INTERPACKET DATA

Any terminating character required by the system can be added at the end of the packet. This is normally a carriage return. It is not considered part of the packet when computing the length or check total. Other characters such as handshaking characters can also be sent between packets.

ERROR CHECKING

There are three ways of computing the CHECK figure, and during initialization the communicating computers must agree upon the method to be used. The receiving program computes the check figure the same way for each packet, and sends a NAK packet if the check figure does not agree with the number in the CHECK field.

Note that the ACK and NAK packets also have check figures and the sending computer should also make sure that the check figures it receives are correct. However, if an ACK or NAK packet has a bad checksum, the sending computer will not send back a NAK. Normally, such a packet is simply ignored and treated as if it were not received.

ONE-CHARACTER CHECKSUM

The simplest CHECK figure to compute is the one-character checksum. It is computed as follows. The ASCII values of all the characters in the block are added up. If the characters are eight-bit, all eight bits are included. Bits 6 and 7 are then added to the number formed by bits 0 through 5. The result is converted into a printable character. Thus, if s is the arithmetic sum of the ASCII characters, then

check = tochar(32 + ((s + ((s AND 192)/64)) AND 63))

TWO-CHARACTER CHECKSUM

For a two-character checksum the arithmetic sum of the characters is computed as a sixteen-bit figure, and the low-order twelve bits are sent as two characters converted using the tochar() function (bits 6 through 11 followed by bits 0 through 5).

THREE-CHARACTER CRC

A sixteen-bit cyclical redundancy check figure is calculated and sent as a sequence of three characters formed by applying the tochar() function to bits 12 through 15, bits 6 through 11, and bits 0 through 5, respectively. See Chapter 10 for more information about CRC calculations.

OPTIONAL KERMIT FEATURES

There are two optional additional features that make Kermit even more useful. Unfortunately, they are not included in all versions of Kermit, and cannot be used on all computers, but they are becoming more readily available.

LONG-PACKET EXTENSION

One optional feature, not included in all versions of Kermit, provides for longer packets than originally specified. A request for long-packet authorization is made by the transmitting device setting capability number 4, which is bit 2 of the first CAPAS character in the initialization packet. A receiving program that is able to use long packets will respond by accepting the request.

The transmitting program can also specify the longest packet it can accept as input. This length is indicated in two bytes, MAXL1 and MAXL2. MAXL1 contains the character represented by

$$32 + (length / 95)$$

MAXL2 contains the character represented by

$$32 + (length \bmod 95)$$

MAXL1 and MAXL2 are contained in the second and third bytes of the last CAPAS byte. If they are missing, but the long-packets bit was set, the default length of 500 is used. The regular MAXL byte must also be set with a length conforming to the original Kermit protocol, since it may not be known until after initialization whether the receiving computer is capable of implementing long packets.

When long packets have been agreed on, an individual packet is treated as a long packet if its LEN field is set to zero. The format of a long packet is shown in Table C.4.

Table C.4: Kermit long-packet formula

OFFSET	CONTENTS	MEANING
0	MARK	Normally ^A to mark start of packet
1	LEN	Set to zero to indicate a long packet
2	SEQ	Sequence number, modulo 64, starting at 0
3	TYPE	Packet type
4	LENX1	Character of (32 + INT (length / 95))
3	LENX2	Character of (32 + (length % 95))
3	HCHECK	Checksum of LEN, SEQ, TYPE, LENX1, LENX2
4 …	DATA	Contents of the packet, if applicable
[end]	CHECK	Checksum of all bytes from LEN on

SLIDING WINDOWS

One complaint about the Kermit protocol is that it is slow when used over long distances because of the need to wait for an acknowledgment after each packet is sent. This can add a considerable overhead, especially when the two computers are at remote locations and other media such as networks intervene. In such cases the waiting time can exceed the transmission time.

To solve this problem, the windowing amendment has been proposed. It enables successive packets to be sent without waiting in between for an acknowledgment. Acknowledgment is still expected in due course, however. Not all communications systems can implement sliding windows (described below), since each computer must have full-duplex capability.

Requesting Sliding Windows

A request for windows is made by setting bit 4 of the first CAPAS byte in the initiation packet. At the same time the window size (i.e., number of data packets to be sent sequentially) is placed in the first field following the last CAPAS byte. The maximum number of packets in a window is 31. The receiving device then indicates to the sender whether it is capable of using this feature.

Since the number of packets in a file can exceed the number of packets allowed in a window, the window is seen as sliding through the file. It moves on when the first packet in the window has been successfully transmitted (i.e., acknowledged by the receiving device). The sliding window concept is illustrated in Figure C.1.

Note that long packets and sliding windows are not mutually exclusive. Table C.5 shows the format of a *send-init* packet when both extensions are being implemented.

Starting the Transfer

The sender transmits the file-header packet in the normal way and waits until it has been acknowledged before sending data packets. This is because the receiving device is presumed to be saving the data to a file, but it cannot do this until the file name has been successfully received as part of the file-header packet.

Transferring Data

On receipt of each packet, the receiving device sends an ACK or NAK message as appropriate. It keeps a list of which packets have been successfully received. Likewise, the sending device keeps a list of which packets have been acknowledged by the receiving device.

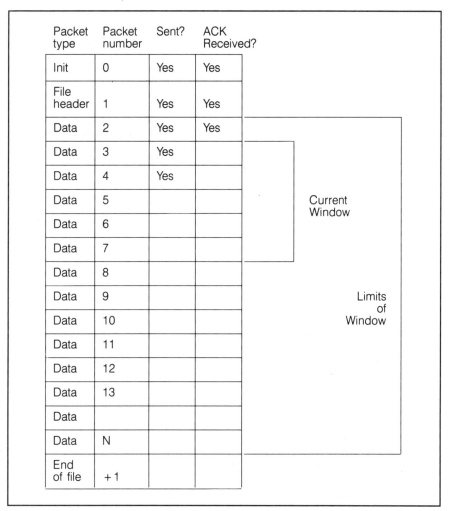

Packet type	Packet number	Sent?	ACK Received?
Init	0	Yes	Yes
File header	1	Yes	Yes
Data	2	Yes	Yes
Data	3	Yes	
Data	4	Yes	
Data	5		
Data	6		
Data	7		
Data	8		
Data	9		
Data	10		
Data	11		
Data	12		
Data	13		
Data			
Data	N		
End of file	+ 1		

Figure C.1: Sliding window concept (sender's point of view)

On receipt of a NAK packet, the packet being referred to is re-transmitted, unless it is outside the current window, in which case the first unacknowledged packet is retransmitted. The latter event occurs if a packet number is damaged.

Table C.5: Send-Init packet with long packets and sliding windows

OFFSET	CONTENTS	MEANING
0	MARK	Normally ^A to mark start of packet
1	LEN	Number of ASCII characters after this field
2	SEQ	Sequence number, modulo 64, starting at 0
3	TYPE	Packet type (see below)
4	MAXL	The maximum length packet that can be received
5	TIME	Time-out time
6	NPAD	The number of padding characters
7	PADC	The control character required for padding
8	EOL	Terminating character if any
9	QTCL	The character preceding control characters
10	QBIN	Character preceding characters over 127
11	CHKT	Check type
12	REPT	Repeated character prefix
13	CAPAS	Capability bit mask
14	WINDW	Number of packets in a window
15	MAXL1	High order (MOD 95) of maximum length
16	MAXL2	Low order (MOD 95) of maximum length
17	CHECK	Checksum

Bad Checksums

One problem with this system is that if a packet is received with a bad checksum, sending a NAK may confuse matters. The NAK could be indicating damage to the packet-number field that caused the bad checksum; in that case the NAK would be for the wrong packet.

Kermit solves this problem by having the sending device ignore any ACK or NAK packets that have a bad checksum. If the receiving device receives a data packet with a bad checksum, it should either send a NAK for the oldest unacknowledged packet, if any, or ignore the bad packet; when the next packet comes it will be clear from the packet number whether one has been lost in the meantime, and a NAK can be sent for the missing one.

Ending the Transfer

The sending device will wait for all the packets to be acknowledged before sending an end-of-file packet. It will then ask for that packet to be acknowledged before sending any further files.

Timeouts

If certain packets are lost, it is possible for each device to be waiting for the other. Accordingly, a sending device should respond to a lengthy gap between receipts by sending the oldest unacknowledged packet, and the receiving device should send a NAK for the oldest unacknowledged packet (if any) or for the next packet due. There should probably also be a limit placed on the number of timeout retries of this type so that the attempt to transfer is abandoned if too many problems occur.

Abandoning File Transfer

A sender can terminate transfer by sending an end-of-file packet with D (for discard) in the data field. A receiver can stop the file transfer by placing an X in the data field of an ACK packet. It can stop all file transfers by placing a Z in the data field. The sender will then send an end-of-file packet with the D in the data field and a sequence number of one greater than the number of the ACK that contains the request to stop.

IMPLEMENTING KERMIT

As you have seen, there are a large number of possible Kermit configurations. However, any implementation you use must be able to support the basic, or "classic," Kermit protocol. It must also recognize any requests for features it does not support, and reject such requests. Accordingly, it is possible to incorporate basic Kermit features into a program without having to worry about how to program CRC error detection or how to implement sliding windows.

FURTHER INFORMATION

You can obtain the full Kermit protocol manual (87 pages) and source code for various versions of Kermit from

Kermit Distribution

Columbia University Center for Computing Activities

612 West 115 Street

New York, NY 10025

A nominal charge is made to cover expenses. I recommend anyone intending to implement Kermit to acquire the official documentation. A fuller treatment of Kermit is contained in the book *KERMIT, A File Transfer Protocol* by Frank da Cruz (Bedford, Mass.: Digital Press, 1987).

GLOSSARY

ACK   Acknowledge, ASCII code 6. Used to acknowledge receipt of a transmission.

acoustic coupler   A modem connected to the telephone network by attachment to the handset of a telephone.

APPC   Advanced Program to Program Communications. A set of IBM standards that enables common data to be processed by a variety of computers within an SNA environment.

ARPANET   A packet switching network operated by the U.S. government.

ASCII   American Standard Code for Information Interchange. A set of numbers from zero through 127 assigned to letters, numbers, punctuation marks, and special characters.

asynchronous communication   A method of communication in which the intervals between characters are of uneven length.

baud rate   The length of the shortest signalling condition or event divided into one second.

BISYNC   Binary Synchronous Communications. An IBM synchronous protocol.

bit   Binary digit. A number that can only have the value 1 or 0.

block mode   A facility, available only on some terminals, whereby data on a screen can be edited locally and transmitted as a block when the user has finished, rather than character by character.

blocking I/O   The situation where a system call to read from a device will wait until data are available or for a specified timeout period before returning. Contrasted with non-blocking, where if no data are available the call returns immediately with a count of zero.

bps   Bits per second. The number of binary digits of information transmitted in one second.

break   A special signal used to interrupt a program.

BSC   Another name for BISYNC.

buffer   An area of memory containing data waiting to be transmitted, or received data waiting to be processed.

bulletin board   An electronic database holding messages that can be read and downloaded by a number of users.

CD   Carrier Detect. Used by a modem to indicate the presence of a carrier signal (line 8 on RS-232 connections).

coaxial cable   A cable consisting of a central wire surrounded by another wire in the form of a cylinder.

CompuServe   An organization that offers a number of services to its subscribers including electronic mail, database, and conference facilities.

computer conferencing   A facility whereby several users can talk to each other simultaneously by sending messages to a central computer that sends the information on to all the users currently on-line.

CRC   Cyclical Redundancy Check. An error-checking method of computing a number from a string of transmitted data that is computed by both the transmitting and receiving device.

CTS   Clear to Send. Secondary handshaking line from DCE to DTE (line 5 in RS-232 connections).

cu   A program that enables a user of a UNIX system to log on to a second system via the serial ports of the first system. Though not part of UUCP it can read some UUCP files.

data bits   The bits forming part of a single group of bits that represent data, as opposed to start, parity, and stop bits.

DCA   Document Content Architecture. A standard data format devised by IBM to enable the same documents to be processed by otherwise incompatible computers.

DCE   Data Communication Equipment. Modems and other intermediate communications devices (distinguished from DTE).

device driver   A section of code that acts as a gateway between the operating system and a physical device such as a serial port.

DIALOG   An organization that provides access to a large number of databases at fees that vary according to the database used.

direct connection   Used in this book to refer to devices connected through RS-232 wires rather than through modems.

DSR   Data Set Ready. Primary handshaking line from DCE to DTE, (line 6 in RS-232 connections).

DTE   Data Terminal Equipment. Terminals and other devices that are the source or final destination of data, as opposed to DCE devices, which are intermediate communications devices.

DTR   Data Terminal Ready. Primary handshaking line from DTE to DCE (line 20 in RS-232 connections).

EBCDIC   Extended Binary Coded Decimal Interchange Code. An alternative to the ASCII code. It is used mainly by IBM computers other than the IBM PC series.

ENQ   Enquiry, ASCII code 5. Used to ask for ACK or NAK.

ENQ/ACK   A handshaking protocol using the ENQ, ACK, and NAK characters.

even parity   Adding a bit after the data bits to make the total number of binary ones in the data bits and the parity bit an even number (*see also* parity check).

forms caching   A facility on some terminals whereby several screens of data can be entered locally, and subsequently transmitted as one batch.

FSK   Frequency Shift Keying. Used by some modems to encode data as different frequencies.

full duplex   Simultaneous two-way communication.

getty   A UNIX program that watches serial ports for activity and allows people to log on.

half duplex   Communication in two directions but not at the same time.

hardware interrupt   A signal sent from a device indicating the occurrence of an event.

HDLC   High Level Data Link Control. A synchronous protocol.

Honey DanBer   A version of UUCP standardized by Peter Honeyman, David Norwitz, and Brian Redman.

Internet   A U.S. Government network linking goverment facilities and academic research centers.

interrupt   *See* hardware interrupt, software interrupt.

I/O   Input/Output.

IP   Internet Protocol, specifying the format of data for transmission on the Internet. Commonly used in conjunction with TCP to form TCP/IP.

ISDN   Integrated Services Digital Network. A system being developed that integrates voice, data, and other communications over common channels.

Kermit   A protocol designed for micro-to-mainframe file transfers. (Also a talking frog.)

LAN   Local Area Network. A system connecting a number of communications devices in one location.

LRC   Longitudinal Redundancy Check. An alternative check to the CRC.

MARK   The communication of a binary 1, represented by a negative voltage in direct connection.

modem   Modulator Demodulator. A device for converting computer communications to and from a form appropriate for the telephone network.

multiplex   A method whereby several devices can share a communications channel.

multipoint   A system where several devices are sharing a single communications line.

NAK   Negative Acknowledge, ASCII code 21 decimal. Used to indicate errors in a received transmission.

network   A system connecting a number of communications devices.

node   A part of a network connected to a number of circuits that are consolidated for onward transmission.

null modem   A set of circuits that enables two DTE or two DCE devices to be connected by swapping the necessary wires.

odd parity   Adding a bit after the data bits so as to make the total number of binary ones in the data bits and the parity bit an odd number (*see also* Parity check).

packet   A group of data elements transmitted together that generally forms part of a larger transmission made up of a number of packets. A packet is made up of additional information such as packet number and error detecting codes.

packet switching   A method of communication that involves splitting a transmission up into packets. Successive packets along a given channel can belong to different transmissions.

PAD   Packet Assembler/Disassembler. A device used to create and unpack packets in packet switching.

PAM   Phase Amplitude Modulation. Used by some modems to translate bits into a combination of phase shifts and frequency changes.

parity bit   A bit sent after the data bits used for error detection. It is computed from the data bits by both the transmitting and receiving devices and the result is then compared.

parity error   The condition that arises when the parity bit does not bear the correct relationship to the data bits.

phase modulation   Used by some modems to translate bits into different phases of a carrier signal.

PIC   Programmable Interrupt Controller. A chip used to enable and prioritize hardware interrupts and pass them on to the CPU.

point-to-point   The opposite of multipoint. A communications line is being used by only one device at each end.

polling   A CPU repeatedly examines a number of devices in turn to see whether anything has happened as opposed to interrupt-driven communications where the devices themselves notify the CPU when something happens.

protocol   A set of standards covering data communications.

PSK   Phase Shift Keying. Used by some modems to encode data as different phase angles.

RI   Ring Indicator. Used by a modem to indicate that it is receiving a call and would be ringing if it were a telephone. (Line 22 in RS-232 connections).

RQS or RTS Request To Send. Secondary handshaking line from DTE to DCE (line 4 in RS-232 connections).

RXD Received Data. The circuit carrying data from DCE to DTE (line 3 in RS -232 connections).

script A sequence of commands used to automate all or part of a communications session, typically consisting strings to wait for and strings to send in reply.

SDLC Synchronous Data Link Control. A bit-oriented synchronous protocol.

serial communications The transmission of data as a sequence of bits.

SG Signal Ground. A common reference point for various circuits (line 7 in RS-232 communications).

site name The name by which an individual computer is addressed. Individuals on a remote computer are addressed via a combination of site name and user-ID.

SNA Systems Network Architecture. A method used by IBM for connecting computers in a network.

software interrupt Software use of a computer's interrupt mechanism to cause the execution of a section of code associated with a particular interrupt number.

SPACE The communication of a binary zero, represented in direct connection by a positive voltage.

special file An entry appearing in a UNIX file directory that contains a pointer to code forming part of the kernel, typically a device driver.

start bit A bit sent in asynchronous communications indicating the start of a new character.

stop bit   A bit sent in asynchronous communications indicating the end of a character.

string   A set of characters transmitted or received together, such as a password.

stty   A program that enables the communications parameters of an open serial port to be modified.

synchronous communications   The transmission of a sequence of data elements at regularly spaced intervals without the use of start and stop bits framing each character.

TCP   Transmission Control Protocol. A protocol used in UNIX networking.

TCP/IP   The combination of TCP and IP.

TDM   Time Division Multiplexing. The use of a single line by several devices, each with its own time slot.

Telenet   A commercial packet-switching network.

timeout   A period after which, if no response is received, an error is considered to have occurred.

TXD   Transmitted Data. The line carrying data from DTE to DCE (line 2 in RS-232 connections).

Tymnet   A commercial packet-switching network.

UART   Universal Asynchronous Receiver/Transmitter. A chip with serial/parallel conversion, parallel/serial conversion, and other facilities designed for use in asynchronous serial communications.

USART   Universal Synchronous/Asynchronous Receiver/Transmitter. It is similar to a UART, but has synchronous capability also.

user-ID   The name given to an individual user of a computer by the system administrator of that computer. Used by the individual to log on to the computer, and by other users to send mail to the individual.

UUCP A set of programs designed to facilitate file transfer and message passing between UNIX systems.

uucico A program forming part of the UUCP package that handles the actual communication between two machines.

uucp A program forming part of the UUCP package that enables files to be transferred between machines.

uudecode A program forming part of the UUCP package that reconverts data converted by uuencode back into 8-bit format.

uuencode A program forming part of the UUCP package that converts 8-bit data into 7-bit format for transmission along a 7-bit channel.

uugetty A version of getty that allows the same port to be used both for dial-out and dial-in.

uuname A program forming part of the UUCP package that lists machines that the local machine can connect to.

uustat A program forming part of the UUCP package that reports on the status of pending UUCP transfers.

uux A program forming part of the UUCP package that requests the execution of commands on a remote system.

VRC Vertical Redundancy Check. The use of odd or even parity as an error-checking mechanism.

WATS Wide Area Telephone Service. Unlimited use of a telephone circuit for specified periods for an agreed charge.

Word length The number of data bits sent at one time during asynchronous communications.

XMODEM A protocol designed for transfers between microcomputers.

X.PC   An asynchronous version of X.25.

X.25   A protocol used by the packet-switching networks.

YMODEM   An enhanced version of XMODEM.

BIBLIOGRAPHY

Anderson, Bart, Bryan Costadeles, and Harry Henderson. *UNIX Communications*. Indianapolis: Hayden Books, 1987.

Bach, Maurice J. *The Design of the UNIX Operating System*. Englewood Cliffs, N.J.: Prentice Hall, Inc., 1986.

Campbell, Joe. *The RS-232 Solution,* second edition. San Francisco: SYBEX, Inc. 1989.

da Cruz, Frank. *Kermit, A File Transfer Protocol*. Bedford, Mass.: Digital Press 1987.

Fielder, David, and Bruce H. Hunter. *UNIX System Administration*. Indianapolis: Hayden Books, 1987.

Frey, Donnalyn, and Rick Adams. *!%@:: A Directory of Electronic Mail Addressing and Networks*. Sebastopol, Calif.: O'Reilly and Associates, 1990.

Gofton, Peter. *Mastering Serial Communications*. San Francisco: SYBEX, 1986.

Kochan, Stephen G., and Patrick H. Wood. *UNIX Networking.* Indianapolis: Hayden Books, 1989.

McNamara, John E. *Technical Aspects of Data Communications*. Bedford, Mass.: Digital Press, 1982.

Rochkind, Marc J. *Advanced UNIX Programming*. Englewood Cliffs, N.J.: Prentice Hall, Inc., 1985.

Todino, Grace. *Using UUCP and Usenet.* Sebastopol, Calif.: O'Reilly and Associates, 1990.

Todino, Grace, and Tim O'Reilly. *Managing UUCP and Usenet*. Sebastopol, Calif.: O'Reilly and Associates, 1990.

INDEX

SYBEX ®

FREE CATALOG!

Mail us this form today, and we'll send you a full-color catalog of Sybex books.

Name _____

Street _____

City/State/Zip _____

Phone _____

Please supply the name of the Sybex book purchased.

_____

How would you rate it?

_____ Excellent   _____ Very Good   _____ Average   _____ Poor

Why did you select this particular book?

_____ Recommended to me by a friend

_____ Recommended to me by store personnel

_____ Saw an advertisement in _____

_____ Author's reputation

_____ Saw in Sybex catalog

_____ Required textbook

_____ Sybex reputation

_____ Read book review in _____

_____ In-store display

_____ Other _____

Where did you buy it?

_____ Bookstore

_____ Computer Store or Software Store

_____ Catalog (name: _____)

_____ Direct from Sybex

_____ Other: _____

Did you buy this book with your personal funds?

_____ Yes   _____ No

About how many computer books do you buy each year?

_____ 1-3   _____ 3-5   _____ 5-7   _____ 7-9   _____ 10+

About how many Sybex books do you own?

_____ 1-3   _____ 3-5   _____ 5-7   _____ 7-9   _____ 10+

Please indicate your level of experience with the software covered in this book:

_____ Beginner   _____ Intermediate   _____ Advanced

Which types of software packages do you use regularly?

_____ Accounting	_____ Databases	_____ Networks
_____ Amiga	_____ Desktop Publishing	_____ Operating Systems
_____ Apple/Mac	_____ File Utilities	_____ Spreadsheets
_____ CAD	_____ Money Management	_____ Word Processing
_____ Communications	_____ Languages	_____ Other _____
		(please specify)

Which of the following best describes your job title?

_____ Administrative/Secretarial	_____ President/CEO
_____ Director	_____ Manager/Supervisor
_____ Engineer/Technician	_____ Other _____
	(please specify)

Comments on the weaknesses/strengths of this book: _____

_____

_____

_____

_____

PLEASE FOLD, SEAL, AND MAIL TO SYBEX

– – – – – – – – – – – – – – – – – – – –

SYBEX, INC.
Department M
2021 CHALLENGER DR.
ALAMEDA, CALIFORNIA USA
94501

SYBEX ®

SEAL

UUCP FILE STRUCTURE

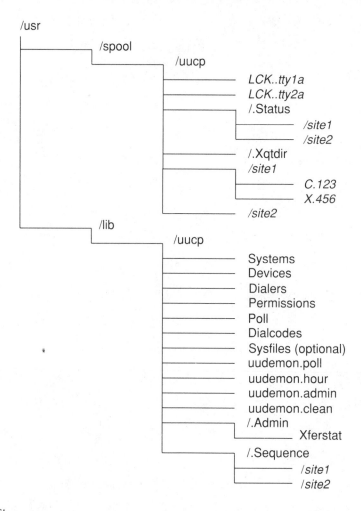

Notes:

1. Entries preceded by / are directories.
2. Entries in italics represent files that will have different names depending on the site or device.
3. LCK.. files only exist when the particular device is in use.